D0359566

Wild Berries
of the West

Betty B. Derig and
Margaret C. Fuller
Illustrated by Mimi Osborne

2001
MOUNTAIN PRESS PUBLISHING COMPANY
Missoula, Montana

Text © 2001 by Betty B. Derig and Margaret C. Fuller

Illustrations © 2001 by Mimi Osborne

Photograph Credits—See page iv

Front cover photograph:
Americanbush cranberries *(Viburnum trilobum)*
© 2001 by Betty B. Derig

Back cover photographs:
Serviceberries *(Amelanchier alnifolia)*,
salmonberries *(Rubus spectabilis)*,
and bittersweet berries *(Solanum dulcamara)*
© 2001 by Betty B. Derig
All rights reserved

DISCLAIMER

The author, publisher, bookseller, and anyone else associated with the distribution of this book assume no liability for the actions of the reader. Use common sense when picking and eating wild berries. Do not eat anything you cannot identify confidently as edible. Many of the fruits and berries included in this book are toxic and should not be ingested. Look for the warning **TOXIC** in the edibility section. Medicinal uses of plants are included as a matter of historical interest, not as a guide to modern herbal medicine.

Library of Congress Cataloging-in-Publication Data
Derig, Betty B.
    Wild berries of the West / Betty B. Derig and Margaret C. Fuller
        p. cm.
    Includes bibliographical references (p.   ).
    ISBN 0-87842-433-4 (alk. paper)
        1. Berries—West (U.S.)—Identification.   2. Cookery (Berries)
    I. Fuller, Margaret, 1935–   II. Title.

QK133.D47 2001
    581.4'64'0978—dc21

2001030669

PRINTED IN HONG KONG BY MANTEC PRODUCTION COMPANY

Mountain Press Publishing Company
P.O. Box 2399 • Missoula, Montana 59806
(406) 728-1900

In memory of our mothers

Hattie Lindgren Carson &
Eleanor Hanford Cathcart

who loved wild berries and old recipes

Photograph Credits

Photographs © 2001 Russ Buhrow: pages 15, 19 (top), 27

Photographs © 2001 Betty B. Derig: pages 7 (top left, bottom), 11, 13, 17, 21, 23, 35 (top), 37, 47, 49 (top inset), 51, 53, 55, 63 (top), 65 (bottom right, bottom left), 79, 81, 85, 87, 89 (bottom), 93 (top, bottom left), 95 (bottom), 97, 98, 103, 107, 111, 113, 115, 120, 121, 123, 127, 129 (top), 131 (bottom), 135 (top, bottom right), 137 (inset), 139, 141, 147, 149 (top left, bottom left, bottom right), 151, 153, 155, 157, 159 (top), 161, 165, 167, 169 (top left), 171, 173 (insets)

Photographs © 2001 Margaret C. Fuller: pages 7 (top right), 31, 33, 39, 41 (bottom), 43, 45, 49 (top, bottom, bottom inset), 57, 59, 63 (bottom), 65 (top), 67, 73, 75, 77, 83, 89 (top), 91, 93 (bottom right), 99, 101 (bottom right), 117, 129 (bottom), 131 (top), 133, 135 (bottom left), 137 (top, bottom), 143, 145, 149 (top right), 159 (bottom), 173 (bottom), 175

Photograph © 2001 Michael Gadomski, Photo Researchers, Inc.: page 41 (top)

Photograph © 2001 James R. Johnson, South Dakota State University: page 118

Photographs © 2001 John Kallas, Wild Food Adventures: pages 61, 101 (bottom left)

Photographs © 2001 Bob Moseley: pages 25, 71, 169 (top right, bottom)

Photograph © 2001 Dan Nickrent, Southern Illinois University at Carbondale: page 105

Photograph © 2001 Richard Parker, Photo Researchers, Inc.: page 163

Photograph © 2001 Jack Ryan, Photo Researchers, Inc.: page 19 (bottom)

Photograph © 2001 Charlene Simpson: page 95 (top)

Photograph © 2001 Gladys Lucille Smith, California Academy of Science: page 101 (top)

Photograph © 2001 Charles Webber, California Academy of Science: page 35 (bottom)

Photograph © 2001 Virginia Weinland, Photo Researchers, Inc.: page 109

Contents

Acknowledgments   *ix*

Introduction   *1*

Wild Berries   *5*

   Barberry Family
      Barberries and Oregon Grapes (*Mahonia* species)   *6*

   Buckthorn Family
      Buckthorns (*Rhamnus* species)   *10*
      Graythorn (*Zizyphus obtusifolia*)   *14*

   Buttercup Family
      Baneberry (*Actaea rubra*)   *16*

   Cactus Family
      Saguaro (*Carnegiea gigantea*)   *18*
      Barrel Cactus (*Echinocactus acanthodes*)   *20*
      Beavertails and Prickly Pears (*Opuntia* species)   *22*

   Crowberry Family
      Crowberry (*Empetrum nigrum*)   *24*

   Crucifixion Thorn Family
      Crucifixion Thorn (*Koeberlinia spinosa*)   *26*

   Cypress Family
      Junipers (*Juniperus* species)   *28*

   Dogwood Family
      Bunchberry (*Cornus canadensis*)   *32*
      Pacific Dogwood (*Cornus nuttallii*)   *34*
      Red Osier Dogwood (*Cornus sericea*)   *36*

   Elm Family
      Netleafed Hackberry (*Celtis reticulata*)   *38*

   Ginseng Family
      Sarsaparilla and Spikenards (*Aralia* species)   *40*
      Devil's Club (*Oplopanax horridum*)   *42*

   Gooseberry Family
      Gooseberries and Currants (*Ribes* species)   *44*

   Grape Family
      Grapes (*Vitis* species)   *52*

   Heath Family
      Pacific Madrone (*Arbutus menziesii*)   *54*
      Manzanitas (*Arctostaphylos*)   *56*
      Wintergreens (*Gaultheria* species)   *60*
      Salal (*Gaultheria shallon*)   *62*

Blueberries and Huckleberries (*Vaccinium* species)   *64*
Cranberries (*Vaccinium* species)   *70*

Holly Family
Hollies (*Ilex* species)   *72*

Honeysuckle Family
Twinberries and Honeysuckles (*Lonicera* species)   *74*
Elderberries (*Sambucus* species)   *78*
Snowberries (*Symphoricarpos* species)   *82*
Viburnums and Highbush Cranberries (*Viburnum* species)   *84*

Laurel Family
California Bay (*Umbellularia californica*)   *88*

Lily Family
Asparagus (*Asparagus officinalis*)   *90*
Queencups (*Clintonia* species)   *92*
Fairybells (*Disporum* species)   *94*
False Solomon's Seals and
      False Lilies of the Valley (*Maianthemum* species)   *96*
Greenbriers (*Smilax* species)   *100*
Twisted Stalks (*Streptopus* species)   *102*

Mistletoe Family
Dwarf Mistletoes (*Arceuthobium* species)   *104*
Mistletoes (*Phoradendron* species)   *106*

Mulberry Family
Mulberries (*Morus* species)   *108*

Nightshade Family
Boxthorns (*Lycium* species)   *110*
Groundcherries (*Physalis* species)   *112*
Bittersweets and Nightshades (*Solanum* species)   *114*

Oleaster Family
Buffaloberries (*Shepherdia* species)   *116*

Palm Family
California Fan Palm (*Washingtonia filifera*)   *120*

Rose Family
Serviceberries (*Amelanchier* species)   *122*
Hawthorns (*Crataegus* species)   *126*
Wild Strawberries (*Fragaria* species)   *130*
Toyon (*Heteromeles arbutifolia*)   *134*
Western Crabapple (*Malus fusca*)   *136*
Indian Plum (*Oemleria cerasiformis*)   *138*
Cherries (*Prunus* species)   *140*
Wild Roses (*Rosa* species)   *144*
Blackberries and Raspberries (*Rubus* species)   *148*
Thimbleberry (*Rubus parviflorus*)   *152*

    Salmonberry (*Rubus spectabilis*)   *154*
    Mountain Ashes (*Sorbus* species)   *156*
  Sandalwood Family
    Comandras (*Comandra* species)   *158*
  Silktassel Family
    Silktassels (*Garrya* species)   *160*
  Soapberry Family
    Western Soapberry (*Sapindus saponaria* var. *drummondii*)   *162*
  Sumac Family
    Smooth Sumac (*Rhus glabra*)   *164*
    Sugarbush (*Rhus ovata*)   *166*
    Squawbush (*Rhus trilobata*)   *168*
    Poison Oak and Poison Ivy (*Toxicodendron* species)   *170*
  Sweet Gale Family
    Wax Myrtles and Bayberries (*Myrica* species)   *172*
  Yew Family
    Western Yew (*Taxus brevifolia*)   *174*

Recipes   *177*
  Beverages   *178*
  Breads   *179*
  Desserts   *183*
  Meats and Vegetables   *190*
  Preserves   *194*
  Salads and Salad Dressings   *197*
  Sauces, Syrups, and Condiments   *200*
  Snacks   *205*
  Wild Crafts   *206*
  Drying Berries   *207*
  Freezing Berries   *208*

Selected Botanical Gardens   *209*

Plant Source Guide   *210*
  USDA Plant Hardiness Zones   *210*

Geographic Glossary of Native American Tribes   *211*

Illustrated Glossary of Plant Parts   *215*

Glossary of Technical Terms   *218*

Bibliography   *222*

Recipe Index   *226*

General Index   *228*

Acknowledgments

We are indebted to the many generous persons who helped us with research, plant identification, photo opportunities, hospitality, and innumerable miscellaneous details. We appreciate each one, including the botanists and writers who have gone before us and who appear in our bibliography. The scholarship of Daniel E. Moerman, author of *Native American Ethnobotany*, and Sandra S. Strike, author of *Ethnobotany of the California Indians*, was critical to our treatment of ethnobotany.

Our community librarians graciously ordered and reordered essential books through interlibrary loan. We are especially grateful to Pat Hamilton at the Weiser Public Library and to Linda Hieb at the Caldwell Public Library.

Various botanical gardens presented a wealth of plants for study and photography. The Rancho Santa Ana Botanic Garden in Claremont, California, was a particularly rich source for plants of the Southwest and for species native to a variety of climates and elevations. The staff was always helpful, and Bart O'Brien and Lydia Newcomb were ongoing sources of information. The University of California Botanical Garden at Berkeley and the Regional Parks Botanic Garden in Tilden Park, Berkeley, provided excellent opportunities to study and photograph California native plants. Curator Holly Forbes of University of California Berkeley Botanical Garden, and Russ Buhrow, grounds curator at Tohono Chul Park, Tucson, were generous in sharing their knowledge of plants.

On the northwest coast, Charlene Simpson, project leader for the Lane County Wild Plant Checklist, guided us to plant locations. Her assistance was critical. Eve Oliver provided bed, breakfast, and botanizing in the Puget Sound area. In Idaho, Greg Lind, botanist with the Boise National Forest, Idaho City Ranger District, was very helpful in assisting with plant identification and nomenclature. Mark Mousseaux and Diane Penny, botanists with the Idaho Panhandle National Forests, provided precise directions to plant locations.

Other persons who provided hospitality or gave generously of their time include Eliene Bundy, Dee Foxgrover, Florence Pobanz, Tom and Debbie Cathcart, Anne Cohen, Leslie Magryta, and Neal Fuller.

Bob Moseley, Charlene Simpson, James R. Johnson, and Dan Nickrent offered plant photos without charge to help us fill in the blank spaces. Mimi Osborne created the beautiful illustrations of special plant characteristics, and Bob Moseley read the manuscript for technical accuracy. We are deeply indebted to all of them.

Not least, we thank our husbands, children, and grandchildren who have been liberal with their help and encouragement.

Queen
Charlotte
Islands

Vancouver
Island

CASCADE RANGE

ROCKY MOUNTAINS

COAST RANGES

SIERRA NEVADA

Great Basin

Mojave
Desert

Sonoran
Desert

Chihuahuan
Desert

Baja

Wild Berries of the West *features plants that grow primarily in
western North America from the Rocky Mountains to the Pacific Coast
as far north as British Columbia and south into northern Mexico.*

Introduction

Wild berries are one of nature's special bonuses. They are a visual delight. Drifts of white or pink blossoms color the landscape in spring, and in late summer ripened berries glow in the sunshine like stained glass. Many berries taste as delicious as they look, and what a bonus for the kitchen if you feel inclined to harvest a few. Does anything smell better than huckleberry pie baking?

Some berries, such as huckleberries, raspberries, and strawberries, are good either raw or cooked. Others, such as elderberries, need to be cooked and sweetened, and still others, such as chokecherries, are not palatable except in jam or jelly. Some are not palatable no matter what you do with them, and a few, like the fleshy caps of western yew, are toxic. We encourage our readers to identify plants before nibbling.

Our book is a field guide for hikers and foragers—it identifies the most common berries of the West. In general, this includes those that grow in the moist Pacific climate, the Cascade Range, the Rocky Mountains, the Great Basin, the Sierra Nevada, the California coastal ranges, and the deserts of the Southwest.

From early times, wild berries of the West have been a major food source for Native Americans and have provided medicine, tools, dyes, and materials for cultural and religious activities. The study of the relationship between plants and people is called ethnobotany. We include as much of this lore as possible because we believe it enriches our appreciation of the plants and the people who used them. We include medicinal uses for many of the plants as a matter of historical interest. We do not recommend the use of any particular plant as medicine.

One of our favorite stories is from an ancient Indian myth. It says that humans killed so many animals in early times that the animals sent diseases to earth in self-defense. Eventually the plants took pity on humans and helped them develop cures for the diseases.

A few of the plant cures that have come to us from ancient tradition are common today. One of these is taking cranberry juice to prevent bladder infections. Other uses from the endless plant pharmacy may seem far-fetched or even humorous. One interesting aspect of plant medicine is that widely separated groups of Native Americans used the same species of plant to treat the same ailments.

Many of the fruits we include in this guide do not meet the botanical definition of a berry—a fleshy fruit developed from a single pistil. Trying to determine which fruit is actually a berry can be confusing. A currant is a true berry. A chokecherry, which has one seed, is a drupe. A blackberry is a mass

1

of tiny drupes and is called an aggregate. A serviceberry shows a seed formation like an apple and is called a pome. The fruit of prickly pear cactus looks nothing like a conventional berry, but it fits one botanist's definition of a berry: "a pulpy fruit with no true stone, such as the tomato." In this guide, we include many true berries and many small fruits that we just think of as berries.

In describing the plants, we use the common name and scientific name for each species and organize them alphabetically by common family name. Species and species groups within a family are organized alphabetically by their scientific genus name. We present general information about the family and more detailed information about each species or species group. We include information on range and habitat, edibility, and Native American uses of the berries.

Toxic or poisonous berries or plant parts are marked with a warning **TOXIC** in the edibility section. We include several naturalized but non-native plants with toxic berries in our book. These writeups will help readers identify what *not* to eat. Because of length considerations, we could not include every non-native plant that has naturalized in the West. For instance, we did not include English ivy (*Hedera helix*), a naturalized species that has toxic berries.

We offer recipes for the better tasting berries. Plants with recipes have a pie icon ⬤ under the edibility heading. The recipes are in a separate section at the back of the book.

We urge our readers to get acquainted with native plants. Visiting a nearby botanical garden is a good place to start as many of them feature regional native plants. We list some of the gardens we have particularly enjoyed in the Selected Botanical Gardens appendix. We recommend *The Garden Tourist* by Lois G. Rosenfeld, an annually updated guide to botanical gardens throughout the United States and Canada.

Many native plants do well in cultivation and provide surprisingly attractive, edible landscaping. Blooms are impressive, and the fruits tempt birds as well as gardeners. Wild plants are also environmentally friendly, flourishing in their natural environment with a minimum of water. Grow them in their proper climatic zone, and water well until they take root. We've described the landscape possibilities for many plants in this book, focusing particularly on those that are not already common or well-known garden plants.

We use the United States Department of Agriculture (USDA) zone system as a guide to hardiness. The zone ratings are based on the ability of plants to survive the average minimum temperatures in winter. Zones are suggestions only, as no zone fully encompasses all the local microclimates existing within a small geographic area, nor accounts for all the whims of Mother Nature. One way to determine if your plants are likely to flourish in the suggested zone is to consult the local county extension agent. Minimum temperatures of USDA zones are listed in the Plant Source Guide.

We recommend buying plants from nurseries that sell only nursery propagated stock. Digging plants and taking cuttings threaten the presence of native plants in the wild. A good selection of native plants or cultivars is usually available from nurseries within their growing range. We list plant nurseries we are familiar within the Plant Source Guide. We are not promoting any particular nursery and provide sources only as a service to our readers. Some of the native plants are very difficult to find.

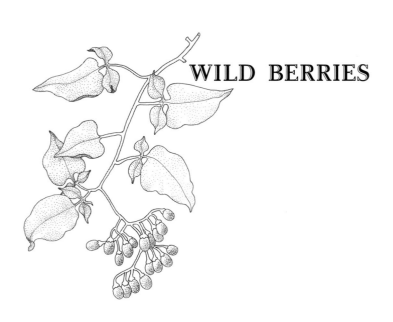

WILD BERRIES

BARBERRY FAMILY   BERBERIDACEAE

The barberry family is composed of sixteen genera that grow in the north and south temperate zones. The Latin name, Berberidaceae, comes from the Arabs, who used a barberry in medieval times and called it "berberys."

Barberries
Oregon Grapes   *Mahonia* species

The *Mahonia* genus contains some two hundred species native to North and South America, Eurasia, and North Africa. These hollylike plants are "living fossils" that developed 20 to 30 million years ago in Tertiary time. *Mahonia* species vary from low and spreading to 10 feet tall. They have spiny, pinnately compound leaves, whorled clusters of yellow flowers, yellow inner wood, and roots containing medicinal alkaloids. Though the genus *Berberis* is often used for Oregon grapes and barberries, *Mahonia* is now the accepted name in western North America. The name honors Bernard McMahon, who recognized the landscaping possibilities of barberry as early as 1796.

Cascade Oregon grape (M. *nervosa*) is a short, stiff-branched, evergreen shrub that grows about 2 feet high. Usually nine to nineteen sets of paired, leathery leaflets grow opposite each other along a common stem—botanists call this a pinnate form, from the Latin *pinna*, which means "feather." Each leaflet has a spiny margin and three prominent veins. The species name, *nervosa*, comes from an Arabic word meaning "veinlike." The leaves are fairly glossy on top, but underneath they are dull with a whitish bloom. Erect clusters of bright yellow flowers open in the spring. By midsummer these mature into fat, juicy berries, dark blue with a silvery bloom, resembling a bunch of grapelets.

Cascade Oregon grape grows in coastal mountains from southern California to British Columbia and east to the eastern side of the Cascade Range. Members of the Lewis and Clark Expedition discovered Cascade Oregon grape near Celilo Falls on the Columbia River in the fall of 1805. At that time it was a species new to science.

Tall Oregon grape (M. *aquifolium*) is an erect, 3- to 5-foot-tall shrub with shiny, dark green leaves that are spiny and pinnately compound. The leaflets, which grow opposite each other on a wiry stem, can number five, seven, or nine—a single terminal leaflet creates the odd number. Each leaflet has one prominent vein down the center. A group of leaflets forms a compound leaf, which grows alternately along the main stem. Characteristic yellow flowers grow either in upright clusters or in hanging racemes. In midsummer, bunches of tart, bluish purple, grapelike berries form. The evergreen leaves may turn red in winter.

Lewis and Clark discovered tall Oregon grape at the Cascades of the Columbia River in the fall of 1805. Meriwether Lewis described the plant while the party camped at Fort Clatsop (in present-day Oregon) during the winter of 1805–6: "The stem . . . is from a foot to 18 inches high and as large as a goosqu[i]ll." This species is now the state flower of Oregon.

          continued on page 8

cade Oregon Grape berries
Mahonia nervosa

Tall Oregon Grape flowers
Mahonia aquifolium

Tall Oregon Grape hybrid with berries   *Mahonia aquifolium*

Tall Oregon grape grows in the northern coastal mountains of California; on the western slopes of the Sierra Nevada; in shady forests throughout Washington, Oregon, southern British Columbia, and northern Idaho; and on the eastern side of the Cascade Range.

Creeping Oregon grape (*M. repens*), also called holly grape, is a common low shrub whose erect or prostrate branches range from 4 inches to 12 inches long. It has five to seven spiny leaflets, either dull or glossy above, and dull with a whitish bloom beneath. Its yellow blossoms grow in elongated racemes. The grapelike fruits are purple with a whitish bloom.

Creeping Oregon grape grows in coniferous forests on the eastern slopes of the Cascade Range and throughout the Great Basin, extending from sagebrush slopes to high rocky ridges. Its range extends north to British Columbia and south through the Rocky Mountains to New Mexico. It often grows in dry forests in the ponderosa, juniper, and Douglas-fir zones.

Fremont's barberry (*M. fremontii*), a scarce desert shrub, grows 3 to 8 feet tall and has stiff, erect branches. Its compound leaves have hollylike leaflets that usually number five or seven, with three to five stout spines along each edge of each leaflet. When mature, the berries are yellow to red in higher elevations, dull brown in the desert.

This drought-tolerant shrub grows in the dry canyons and foothills of the Sonoran and Mojave Deserts, and below the juniper/pinyon zone in New Mexico and Arizona.

Edibility: Oregon grapes are edible but intensely bitter. The root is a potent medicine and can be **TOXIC**.

 Oregon Grape Jelly, page 195

Historical Uses: Native Americans who gathered the bitter Oregon grape berries often combined them with salal or some other berry that acts as a natural sweetener. They usually boiled, mashed, dried, and stored the mixture of berries for future use. The combined juices were also diluted with water for a refreshing, warm weather "coke."

Roots, stems, and leaves were used medicinally for their berberine content and were often more in demand than the berries. Native Americans from many different geographic regions used various species of Oregon grape for similar ailments. They apparently learned by trial and error that berberine has antibiotic and analgesic properties. The Salish tribes of coastal Washington, the Kootenay and Flathead of the Rocky Mountains, the Shoshone and Paiute of the Great Basin, and the Hopi and Navajo of the southwestern deserts made decoctions of roots and bark to treat multiple ailments. A drink of the diluted decoction was particularly popular as a tonic and blood purifier. Some of the Southwestern tribes knew creeping Oregon grape as *Yerba de la Sangre*, herb of the blood. They also ingested a root decoction for digestive problems, kidney and liver ailments, as a mild laxative, and to relieve the aches and pains of rheumatism. The Navajo used *Mahonia* species to cure scorpion bite and to remove bad luck.

Native Americans steeped roots, stems, or bark for a tealike infusion to use externally as a soothing wash to bathe sore eyes and as an antiseptic for skin sores. They mashed or chewed roots and stems, placing them on wounds to promote healing. Some tribes used the tea as an aperitif.

Native Americans not only gathered *Mahonia* species for medicinal uses, they also extracted a yellow dye that came from the berberine of the inner wood. It was the best dye for many things, and if Oregon grape did not grow locally, native peoples traded for it. They used the brilliant yellow dye for basketry materials, particularly beargrass (*Xerophyllum tenax*), and decorative ornaments such as porcupine quills. Yellow designs brightened buckskin clothing, moccasins, and ceremonial objects. The Karok of northern California believed the berries were poisonous but ingeniously pounded them fresh, with larkspur flowers and salmon glue, to make a durable purple paint for decorating bows and arrows. Today, Oregon grape is used to dye rags for braided rugs.

Pioneers used the fresh berries in desserts, drinks, jam, and wine, and also used the plant as a medicine. According to the Doctrine of Signatures—a belief that a plant's physical characteristics hinted at what disease it was good for—the yellow flowers and yellow wood indicated usefulness for treating jaundice and gallstones. A syrup of berries was given for dysentery and fevers. Great care was taken in using *Mahonia* root as it is very potent and can be toxic.

Oregon grape was listed in the *United States Pharmacopoeia* from 1905 to 1916 and on the National Formulary from 1916 to 1937. Berberine salts are used in modern eyedrops and eye washes, and in Germany, tall Oregon grape bark extract is currently marketed for psoriasis.

Wild Gardening: Oregon grape has been a popular landscaping plant since Thomas Jefferson grew it at Monticello around 1796. Showy clusters of yellow blossoms shine in May and June; plump purple berries with a silvery bloom ripen in midsummer; and the lustrous evergreen, hollylike leaves are attractive year-round. Tall Oregon grape is drought tolerant, remarkably free of pests and diseases, and hardy to USDA zone 5. Cascade Oregon grape and creeping Oregon grape are hardy to USDA zone 4. Nurseries can usually provide a number of Oregon grape species as well as desirable horticultural varieties.

BUCKTHORN FAMILY   RHAMNACEAE

The buckthorn family is composed of about fifty-five genera and nine hundred species of often thorny shrubs and trees that grow in temperate and tropical regions around the world. Some species bear edible fruits; others are better known as sources of dyes and drugs. Several species are grown as ornamentals.

Buckthorns   *Rhamnus* species

The 125 species of *Rhamnus* are mainly tropical. These shrubs or small trees can be evergreen or deciduous with alternate branches that range from flexible to rigid. Some species have thorny twigs. Leaves are simple, alternate or opposite along the stem, and sometimes clustered on short shoots. Flowers may form in umbels or singly and produce a drupe with two to four stones.

California coffeeberry (*R. californica*), usually a rounded, evergreen shrub, may be a 4-foot-tall, spreading bush or may reach a height of 12 feet or more. It has grayish brown or reddish bark, and its dark green leaves are oblong to elliptic and 1 to 4 inches long. The leaf margins may be smooth or finely toothed. Leaves are usually hairless above and paler green beneath and downy, though characteristics vary depending on climate and crossbreeding. Umbels of minute, greenish yellow flowers bloom from April to June. The star-shaped blossoms have five pointed petals and five stamens. Clusters of drupes—berrylike fruits— ripen in early summer when they turn red, black, or the color of coffee. Ripe berries can also be green.

California coffeeberry grows in sandy and rocky sites along the coast and in canyons and on hillsides throughout the coastal ranges from southern Oregon to California and Baja, Mexico. It also grows below 3,500 feet on the western slopes of the Sierra Nevada, in the mountains of the Mojave Desert, and in Utah, Colorado, New Mexico, and Arizona.

Alderleaf buckthorn (*R. alnifolia*), a deciduous shrub, grows only about 3 feet high. Its umbels have one to three flowers, and its berries are black when ripe.

Alderleaf buckthorn likes swampy places at elevations of 4,000 to 7,000 feet. It inhabits the Sierra Nevada and ranges north to Washington and east to the Atlantic Coast.

Redberry (*R. crocea*) looks quite different from California coffeeberry. It is a stiff shrub with spiny branches and evergreen leaves that often grow in bunches. The leaves are either smooth or slightly hairy and 1 inch or less long. Yellowish green flowers grow in clusters in the leaf axils from March to May. The tart, red berry matures from June to September.

Redberry usually grows below 3,000 feet in coastal sage scrub, chaparral, and mixed evergreen forests in California coast ranges from Lake County to San Diego.

Cascara (*R. purshiana*) is a deciduous shrub or small tree up to 30 feet tall with smooth, silver gray, bitter-tasting bark. The oblong, dark, glossy leaves are alternate though nearly opposite. They measure 2 to 6 inches long and

California Coffeeberry fruit   *Rhamnus californica*
Inset: California Coffeeberry flowers   *Rhamnus californica*

California Coffeeberry fruit   *Rhamnus californica*

are deeply veined, with smooth or finely toothed margins. Inconspicuous, greenish yellow flowers bloom in late spring from stalked umbels that grow in the axils of the leaves or at the ends of branches. Each cluster may contain as many as twenty-five tiny, five-petaled flowers. Small, usually two-seeded, purplish black berries ripen in August and September.

Cascara grows along the Pacific Coast and east of the Cascade Range, particularly in Idaho, Montana, southern Utah, New Mexico, and Arizona. It likes shady sites in mixed woods at low to middle elevations. Lewis and Clark discovered cascara along the Clearwater River in Kamiah Valley, Idaho, in 1805.

Edibility: Cascara berries are edible but taste bland to bitter and can be a severe purgative. The most useful part of cascara is the bark. California coffeeberries are dry and inedible, but the bark has the same laxative qualities as cascara, though in diminished strength. The fruit of redberry is tart but edible.

Historical Uses: Many Native Americans used coffeeberry for medicinal purposes. A decoction made from crushed leaves and bark seems to have been a universal treatment for constipation, colds, and flu symptoms, and was also used as a wash to soothe poison oak rash. The natives applied sap from a broken twig to warts and skin infections and inhaled smoke from burning branches to relieve headaches and rheumatic pain. California tribes often ate the fruits of redberry with meat, but most persons used them as a laxative. Alderleaf buckthorn resembles coffeeberry in medicinal properties.

Cascara has been the all-American laxative for more than one hundred years, though Native Americans have been well acquainted with its laxative properties for even longer. The Nez Perce introduced cascara to Lewis and Clark, who returned East with samples of bark. *United States Pharmacopoeia* has listed it as a medicine since 1890. Though several species of cascara are laxatives, pharmaceutical companies prefer *R. purshiana*. So much bark has been collected in British Columbia, Washington, Oregon, and California that numbers of wild trees have been significantly diminished.

Writer Jeff Hart says that the Flathead of Montana believe the mode of cascara harvest is important. If the bark is stripped downward, the drug acts as a purgative. If stripped upward, it becomes an emetic. One tribal member challenged him, "And if you don't believe it, then try it yourself and you'll find out."

Wild Gardening: Coffeeberry, a lush and tropical-looking plant with leathery, evergreen leaves and colorful fruits, grows in USDA zone 7. Cascara's valuable ornamental qualities include prominently veined leaves that turn yellow in fall and berries that become purplish black at maturity. It grows best in USDA zones 5 and 6.

Cascara fruit   *Rhamnus purshiana*

Redberry fruit   *Rhamnus crocea*
Inset: Redberry flowers   *Rhamnus crocea*

Graythorn   *Zizyphus obtusifolia*

Graythorn is also known by the scientific name *Condalia lycioides*. *Condalia* and *Zizyphus* species tend to interbreed and change form and foliage in different climates, so botanists do not always agree on the classification. The *Zizyphus* genus includes about one hundred species of thorny trees and shrubs that were formerly included in the *Condalia* genus.

Graythorn, a scraggly, gray-barked, deciduous shrub, grows 3 feet high. Its branches alternate on the stem and may be smooth but often have patches of short, white hairs. Its 1- to 3-inch-long twigs are thorn tipped. Deciduous leaves are ovate, ½ to 1 inch long, and covered with fine hairs. Leaf margins may be smooth or toothed. In spring, clusters of yellowish flowers bloom in cymes or small panicles. Individual flowers have five petals and five sepals, each ⅛ inch long. The ¼ inch-diameter, bluish black drupes have a single stone.

Graythorn grows in creosote bush scrub from 1,500 to 4,500 feet elevation in southeastern Arizona, New Mexico, western and central Texas, and northeastern Mexico.

Edibility: Graythorn fruits are edible but vary from palatable to bitter and from juicy to dry.

Historical Uses: To avoid the fierce thorns, southwestern Native Americans beat the berries off the bushes with sticks and gathered them in baskets. They ate the berries fresh or mixed them with meat into pemmican. Sometimes the berries were dried, ground into meal, and stored for winter use. The Comanche and Apache used a decoction of bark and roots as an antiseptic and to relieve pain, rubbing it on their horses as well as on themselves. The abundant thorns were used as acupuncture needles to prick the skin around arthritic joints and sprains.

Graythorn immature fruit   *Zizyphus obtusifolia*
—RUSS BUHROW PHOTO

BUTTERCUP FAMILY   RANUNCULACEAE

The buttercup family is composed of some thirty-five genera and more than one thousand species of herbs and shrubs that grow mainly in the temperate and arctic regions of the Northern Hemisphere. Many genera are poisonous if eaten, though some have medicinal properties. The family includes many common ornamentals such as delphinium, clematis, anemone, and trollius.

Baneberry   *Actaea rubra*

Baneberry is a herbaceous, bushy perennial with long, wiry stems that reach 12 to 30 inches tall. The dark green compound leaves are divided into groups of two or three coarsely toothed, lobed leaflets that range from 3 to 8 inches long. The leaflets are sparse toward the tip of the stem, but at the bottom of the stem they are crowded, resembling basal leaves but not technically growing from the root. In spring, puffy racemes of small, white flowers appear at the tips of the long stems. In late summer, the flowers mature into elongated clusters of bright red or white berries. Plants with all red berries often grow side by side plants with all white berries. The tiny black dots on the white berries suggest another common name, doll's eyes—they resemble the eyes of old-fashioned dolls. White baneberry (*Actaea pachypoda*), which is native to eastern North America, has only white berries. In dry years, baneberry may not set fruit.

Baneberry grows in moist woodlands from the San Bernardino Mountains of southern California north to Washington, Oregon, British Columbia, and Idaho. It also grows in subalpine meadows in the Rocky Mountains as far south as New Mexico.

Edibility: All parts of baneberry are **TOXIC**. The rootstalk can be a violent purgative and emetic and should be left strictly alone.

Historical Uses: Several Indian tribes, including the Blackfeet and Cheyenne, dried the potent roots and made decoctions that were used for washing sores, for coughs and colds, and as gynecological aids for nursing mothers. The Quinault of the Olympic Peninsula chewed the leaves and spit them on boils to promote healing. Leading contemporary herbalist Michael Castleman finds a root tincture useful as an analgesic and liniment for painful sprains.

The Snohomish of coastal Washington dug the roots after the berries matured, cooked them on hot rocks, and ate them with whale oil.

Wild Gardening: Baneberry does well in natural plantings where bold clumps intermingle with ferns, primroses, and other shade-tolerant plants. The cheerful white blossoms put on a spring show, and the berries shine like candles in the shady garden of late summer. Baneberry grows across temperate North America and is hardy to USDA zone 4.

Baneberry flower   *Actaea rubra*

...eberry white berries   *Actaea rubra*   Baneberry red berries   *Actaea rubra*

CACTUS FAMILY   CACTACEAE

The cactus family has more than fifty genera and perhaps fifteen hundred species. They are mostly native to drier, tropical and subtropical regions of North and South America. Many have showy flowers and are popular ornamentals. Cacti are perennial, herbaceous or woody, succulent plants. The stems are columnar or flattened. Cacti do not have leaves, but the green stems photosynthesize. The stems are often jointed and have straight or hooked spines. Solitary flowers have numerous stamens and numerous outer sepals that intergrade with the inner petals to make overlapping rows. The fruit is fleshy.

Saguaro   *Carnegiea gigantea*

Gigantea is an appropriate species name for saguaro—it can grow 30 to 40 feet tall. The spiny, columnar trunk usually bears several erect branches well above its base. Its trunk and branches are prominently ribbed and armed with straight spines. The shallow roots spread far to soak up desert rains, and the body of the plant expands to hold the moisture until needed. In May and June, the saguaro produces exquisite white flowers that bloom only at night. They are about 4 inches long, 2 or 3 inches wide, and form clusters at the ends of the branches. A month after flowering the fruits ripen. The plump, red or purple berries are 2¼ to 3½ inches long, with red pulp and innumerable black seeds.

Saguaro grows about 1 foot every 2 or 3 years and may not produce fruit until it is 30 to 40 years old. It can live for 150 years or more and can develop as many as fifty upraised arms or branches.

This unusual succulent plant is about 90 percent water, but an interior skeleton of woody tissue forms long strands inside the trunk. The strands grow close together at the base of the plant and spread outward toward the top. When the plant dies, the soft tissue deteriorates and exposes the woody tissue, which forms hard, upright rods.

Saguaro likes warm, gentle slopes along arroyos where it gets as much moisture as possible from the infrequent rains. It grows in the Sonoran Desert of northwestern Mexico, Arizona, and southeastern California at elevations from 3,500 to 4,500 feet.

Edibility: Saguaro fruits are delicious and taste crisp and sweet like watermelon.

Historical Uses: Saguaro has been one of the principal foods of the Papago and Pima of Arizona. The Papago dated the New Year from the fruiting of this giant cactus, and the Pima called July the Saguaro Harvest Moon. Because the fruits are very high on the trunk, the Indians used long poles—made from woody saguaro rods lashed together with a hook on top—to bring down the fruit. They ate it fresh or made syrup or preserves, which they stored in clay jars. Some fruits were dried in the sun like figs, becoming candied in their own sugar. Others were left to ferment into a strong liquor. The Papago made butter from the black, oily seeds.

Saguaro is the state flower of Arizona. Saguaros are protected in Saguaro National Park near Tucson, Arizona. State law protects them from vandalism elsewhere. The Papago harvest saguaro fruits on their reservation in Arizona.

Saguaro flowers   *Carnegiea gigantea* —*RUSS BUHROW PHOTO*

Saguaro fruit
Carnegiea gigantea
—*JACK RYAN PHOTO,
PHOTO RESEARCHERS, INC.*

Barrel Cactus
Echinocactus acanthodes
(Ferocactus cylindraceus)

Young barrel cacti are globular but as they age, they grow cylindric and can reach 6 feet or more tall. Stems are erect, ribbed, and armed with stout, hooked spines that are white, pink, or yellowish. Sometimes one or two branches form near the base. The yellow flowers are 1½ to 3 inches long and funnel shaped. The greenish, oval fruit is about 1½ inches long and covered with hairs.

Barrel cactus grows on rocky slopes and gravelly fans below 5,000 feet. It inhabits creosote bush scrub and Joshua tree woodlands in the Mojave Desert and parts of Utah, Arizona, and southern California.

Edibility: The barrel cactus has edible fruits that you can make into cactus candy.

 Cactus Candy, page 186

Historical Uses: Barrel cactus has long been famous as a water source for parched desert travelers, but obtaining the cactus water is not an easy task. You must first slice off the top of the barrel and scoop the pulp out from behind the spiny rind. Then let the pulp drain or pound it to release water. This is a painfully long process for anyone who is parching in the desert sun. However, survivalists still teach this potentially lifesaving procedure. Hungry desert travelers also ate the pulp and the fruit.

Native Americans probably used the barrel cactus more frequently as a cooking pot than for either water or food. After the flesh was scooped out, the remaining barrel made a useful vessel. Hot stones were placed in the pot with the food, and it was probably as convenient as cooking in a woven basket. When the camp was moved, they could leave the cactus pot behind and make a new one at the next camp.

Native Americans used the needle-sharp spines of the barrel cactus for awls and for pricking face and body tattoos. To make awls, they set the spines in heads of hard pitch.

Barrel Cactus *Echinocactus acanthodes*

Beavertails
Prickly Pears

Opuntia **species**

The genus *Opuntia* has perhaps three hundred species, many of which are difficult to identify because of natural hybridization. They are often categorized as prickly pears, beavertails, and chollas. Beavertails and prickly pears have flat joints and edible fruits while chollas have cylindrical stems and joints and produce nothing edible. Many species of *Opuntia*, particularly prickly pears, grow throughout the arid West.

Beavertail cactus (*O. basilaris*) is a low, spreading plant, with flat pads that resemble a beaver's tail. The pads are about 4 to 8 inches long and 2½ to 5 inches wide. They are often greenish purple and covered with indentations that are filled with short, brown bristles. The flowers are usually rose colored and grow at the upper edges of the joints. The spineless, oblong fruits are about 1½ inches long and brownish and dry when ripe.

Beavertail inhabits dry benches and fans below 6,000 feet in creosote bush scrub, Joshua tree woodlands, and in the Mojave and Sonoran Deserts, the Great Basin, and Arizona.

Prickly pear (*O. occidentalis*) is erect or spreading with fleshy stems composed of one to several flattened, oval pads connected at joints. Prickly pear can grow in masses up to 3 feet high and 8 feet wide. The pads have slender spines growing from small indentations. Some spines grow outward, and usually two or more spread downward. The yellow flowers are 2 to 3 inches wide and mature into pear-shaped, spiny, reddish purple fruits.

This species of prickly pear grows on dry fans and washes below 2,000 feet in coastal sage scrub and chaparral in the coastal ranges from southern California to Baja.

Edibility: Despite the unfriendly appearance, the entire prickly pear and beavertail cacti are edible raw or cooked, from the sweet, vitamin-rich fruit to the succulent pads.

 Prickly Pear Syrup, page 204

Historical Uses: Native Americans and European settlers valued the prickly pears for food and medicine. They peeled and ate the ripe fruits, called tunas after singeing off the spines. Sometimes they boiled the fruit to make syrup or candy. Spanish settlers reduced the syrup to a popular thick, dark paste called *queso de tuna*. They also gathered the young pads, or *nopales*, before the spines hardened and ate them as a delectable steamed vegetable. They cooked the young green fruits like applesauce. The fully ripe fruits of many *Opuntia* species were usually dried and the seeds winnowed out and stored. Later they ground the seeds into flour to make a mush. The Spanish also boiled and crushed mature pads to form a sticky juice. Whitewash stuck more securely to adobe walls when mixed with this juice.

The ripe fruits of beavertail cactus are too dry to eat raw, but the young fruits, which are easily broken off with a stick, are enjoyable. Native Americans brushed off the fine, short bristles with twigs and cooked the cleaned fruits in stone-lined pits. In the Panamint Mountains west of Death Valley, the natives used not only the young fruits but also the flower buds and the young, fleshy pads. After removing the spines, they dried the pads in the sun. The pads would then keep indefinitely and later could be boiled and eaten with salt.

Opuntia species have medicinal uses, too. Native Americans scraped the pulp from mature pads and applied it as a wet dressing to cuts and wounds. Sometimes the pads were split, soaked, and used as poultices. Modern herbalists recommend *Opuntia* juice as an emollient, applied topically on dry or irritated skin, or taken internally as a diuretic or to soothe the digestive tract.

Today, prickly pear is grown commercially and widely marketed throughout the Southwest as a popular regional food.

Wild Gardening: *Opuntia* species grow well in dry sites and are excellent for xeriscaping. Some are winter hardy to USDA zone 5.

Top right: Prickly Pear flowers   *Opuntia* species
Bottom right: Prickly Pear fruit   *Opuntia* species
om left: Beavertail Cactus flowers   *Opuntia basilaris*

CROWBERRY FAMILY   EMPETRACEAE

All species of the three genera of the crowberry family are low, evergreen shrubs that grow in cold temperate regions. Deep grooves score the undersides of the needlelike leaves whose edges roll under. A joint divides the leaf blade from the leafstalk. The three petals and three sepals of the flowers are often identical. Male and female flowers form on different plants. The female flower produces a drupe with two to nine seeds.

Crowberry   *Empetrum nigrum*

This low, evergreen plant—one of five *Empetrum* species—has needlelike, dark green leaves about ¼ inch long, similar in size and shape to those of pink mountain heather *(Phyllodoce empetriformis)*. The curved-under leaves are arranged close together on woolly stems, alternately or in whorls of four. Minute, pinkish purple flowers form at the leaf bases or in clusters at the ends of stems in June and July, which is very early in the growing season in their high mountain or sea cliff habitats. Three bracts, the same shape and color as the three sepals, are attached just below the sepals. There are no petals. Purplish or black pea-size berries form both singly and in clusters. They are juicy, but the nine seeds are large and hard.

    The name *Empetrum* is from the Greek *en petros*, meaning "on rock," referring to one of this genus's several habitats. It grows in exposed rocky places, open forests, swamps, and muskegs, preferring peaty or sandy soil. It inhabits northern latitudes around the world. In the United States, crowberry grows in Alaska, in alpine habitats south to the Cascade Range, and on oceanside cliffs as far south as northern California.

Edibility: Crowberries are edible raw or cooked but are sour and taste like the smell of turpentine. Cooking lessens the bad taste but doesn't soften the seeds.

Historical Uses: The Eskimos made a dessert of crowberries and fish paste, but tribes of the western United States seldom ate the seedy berries. Because crowberry is limited to high elevations and northern latitudes, native people in British Columbia and Alaska were most likely to eat them. The Carrier of interior British Columbia gathered crowberries in winter from under the snow, mashed and cooked them in bark troughs, and spread them out to dry. The berries remain on the bush all winter, so Indians sought them during famine. Settlers and sailors used them to prevent scurvy.

Wild Gardening: Crowberry grows well in the rock garden and as groundcover in the peaty soil of a rhododendron garden. It is a vigorous, shade-loving plant and hardy in USDA zones 2 to 7.

Crowberry fruit *Empetrum nigrum*
—BOB MOSELEY PHOTO

CRUCIFIXION
THORN FAMILY   KOEBERLINIACEAE

Not all botanists are in agreement about the status of Koeberliniaceae. Sometimes it is classified as Papaveraceae. *Koeberlinia* is the only genus in the family and it contains only one species—*Koeberlinia spinosa.*

Crucifixion Thorn   *Koeberlinia spinosa*

Crucifixion thorn of North America is not the Biblical crucifixion thorn, *Holocanatha emoryi.* Our crucifixion thorn is a well-armed shrub or tree that grows 20 feet tall. The stout branches often form a tangled, spiny thicket. The minute leaves, which fall when climatic conditions become too hot or dry, are alternate, scalelike, and simple. The stems and spine-tipped branches continue to photosynthesize after the leaves drop—an adaptation to desert conditions. The mass of thorny branches gives the shrub an unpromising look, but it produces umbels of tiny yellowish flowers ¼ inch or less in diameter from March to October. The flowers mature into clusters of sweet, black berries.

In the northern Chihuahuan Desert in southern New Mexico, roots of crucifixion thorn grow to a depth of 12 to 16 feet, or until they encounter hard layers of earth. Then they turn and grow straight up. With deeply penetrating roots and upward growing roots near the soil surface, the plant takes advantage of small amounts of desert rain and soil moisture.

Crucifixion thorn inhabits creosote bush scrub and riparian woodlands in mountain canyons and gravelly mesas from 2,400 to 5,000 feet elevation. It grows in central and eastern Arizona, the Chihuahuan Desert of southern New Mexico, the coastal plain of Texas, and the along the Rio Grande.

Edibility: The fruit of crucifixion thorn is sweet and edible.

Historical Uses: Native Americans of the Southwest who were willing to dodge the thorns gathered the fruits.

Crucifixion Thorn berries   *Koeberlinia spinosa*
—RUSS BUHROW PHOTO

Cypress Family   Cupressaceae

Plants of the cypress family are pitchy, evergreen shrubs and trees. The 21 genera and 130 species include such resinous, coniferous trees as junipers, cypresses, and cedars. These trees have no flowers or fruits, only female seed cones and male pollen cones. The leaves are either small scales or shaped like tiny ice picks. Each cone bears several unfertilized seeds. The female cones are either woody (cypresses) or fleshy, like berries (junipers).

Junipers   *Juniperus* species

All sixty species of aromatic, evergreen juniper trees and shrubs grow in the Northern Hemisphere. Scalelike or awl-like leaves grow opposite each other or in whorls on the twigs. Both female and male flowers are minute—the male flowers are mainly stamens and the female flowers are pointed scales. Junipers differ from other conifers in that the cone scales on the female tree are fused and fleshy, resembling bluish berries that mature in their second year. Male trees produce pollen cones.

Rocky mountain juniper (*J. scopulorum*) is a graceful tree that can grow more than 30 feet tall and be 3 feet in diameter at the trunk. Its scaly bark is divided into narrow, gray ridges with younger, reddish brown bark between the ridges. Female trees have mainly shreddy bark and male trees have mainly peeling, patchy bark. The leaves are grayish green to dark green scales, the color depending on the thickness of the waxy coating. This scaly type of leaf is a water-saving adaptation to a dry climate. The leaves have smooth edges and are usually opposite, arranged in twos. Juvenile leaves are needles, rather than scales.

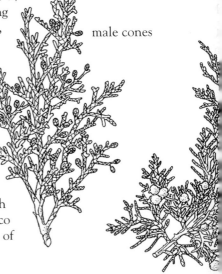

male cones

female cone

Cones appear every two years. Male trees produce tiny brownish cones about ¼ inch long that have scales containing pollen. Female cones are ¼-inch-wide, bright blue "berries" covered with a whitish bloom. They are not true berries but instead are fleshy cone scales fused together. They form in May or June but don't mature until the following year. Mature berries may lose the white bloom.

Rocky Mountain juniper grows on dry, rocky ridges in foothills and lower valleys from British Columbia and Alberta south through the Rocky Mountains to New Mexico and Arizona. It has the widest range of any treelike juniper in the West.

Common juniper (J. communis), a creeping shrub, has needlelike leaves instead of scales. The berries are bluish black and covered with a white bloom. The tops of the needles have a groove with a white line in it, and the bottoms have a keel. Whorls of three needles are joined to the stem by winglike extensions. Common juniper grows around the world in northern latitudes.

Western juniper (J. occidentalis), also called Sierra juniper, is a large tree with fibrous, cinnamon-colored bark and egg-shaped, bluish black berries. Its branches often spread at right angles, forming a flat top. The leaves are grayish green or dark green scales that overlap. In the center of each one is a white dot of resin or a recess formed by a resin gland. The large amount of resin makes the foliage very pungent. The leaves look toothed under a twenty-power lens, but you cannot see the teeth with the naked eye or with a less powerful lens. The fruit has a whitish bloom and is about ⅓ inch across.

Western juniper grows in sagebrush areas and juniper woodlands in the Sierra Nevada, northeastern California, northeastern Oregon, southwestern Washington, and a few places in southwestern Idaho.

California juniper (J. californica) resembles western juniper, but its bark is gray and the berries are up to ¾ inch across and reddish brown instead of blue. California juniper prefers dry woodlands up to about 6,000 feet elevation. Widespread in the foothills of California, it also grows in southern Nevada, northwestern Arizona, and Baja.

Utah juniper (J. osteosperma) has a crooked trunk, ash gray to brown bark, and light yellowish green leaves. The tree is about 10 feet tall. Its berries are bluish to reddish brown beneath a whitish bloom. Utah juniper grows in much of Utah, Nevada, and Arizona, and in western Colorado, western New Mexico, southwestern Wyoming, and southeastern Idaho.

One-seed juniper (J. monosperma) grows about 10 feet tall with branches at the ground. Its bark is fibrous and shredding, and its leaves are yellowish green scales. The range for one-seed juniper includes Utah, Arizona, and New Mexico, plus southeastern Nevada, southwestern Colorado, and western Texas.

Alligator-bark juniper (J. deppeana) has bark divided into rectangular or square plates. It has both scalelike and needlelike leaves, and the berries are light brown. It grows mainly in Arizona.

Edibility: Juniper berries are edible but have the odd flavor of gin. The juicy berries of one-seed juniper taste particularly bad. Some authors say juniper berries are toxic, especially for children or when eaten frequently or in large quantities. However, using a few for flavoring for meats or stews or for gin is acceptable. The extract of juniper leaves, oil of juniper, is **TOXIC**.

Bill's Juniper-Sauerkraut Casserole, page 192
Juniper Chicken and Biscuits, page 193

Historical Uses: Native Americans had many uses for the wood, bark, and leaves of juniper, but few of them ate the berries unless food was scarce. The tribes of central and southeastern California dried juniper berries and ground them into meal for making mush or bread.

Natives frequently used juniper for medicines. From the Nez Perce in Idaho to the Navajo of Arizona, juniper tea was a treatment for colds, coughs, headaches, and flu. The Paiute of the Great Basin liked to boil the berries, skim off the pitch, and drink what was left or inhale the fumes. Juniper medicine took a harsher form among the Maidu and Yuki of California. To treat sinus congestion, they made a hole in the septum of the nose and inserted a juniper twig.

Native women often used juniper as a gynecological aid. Shoshone women periodically drank juniper berry tea as a contraceptive. Native women, as well as pioneer women, used the tea to induce abortions, sometimes with fatal results, as juniper oils increase uterine contractions. Pregnant Zuni and Apache women in the ninth month drank juniper tea daily to promote muscle relaxation during labor.

From 1820 to 1947, the *United States Pharmacopoeia* listed juniper oil as a diuretic. Modern scientific data shows that juniper berries have antiviral and anticancer properties.

Indians often made utensils and tools from the light, soft, durable wood. The decorative wood is naturally streaked red and white. During illness and after a death, the Pueblo as well as tribes of interior British Columbia burned juniper wood to fumigate their dwellings with smoke. The oil in the wood readily burns and forms an aromatic smoke. The Navajo made green dye from juniper bark and berries and burned the wood to make charcoal powder for sand paintings. Shredded juniper bark was useful for diapers, rope, and tinder. As late as the 1940s, women of the San Ildefonso Pueblo near Santa Fe, New Mexico, still gathered bark for diapers.

Juniper had ceremonial and psychological uses, too. The Navajo carried a sprig of it at night to protect against ghosts and evil spirits. Cheyenne men carved juniper wood flutes, hoping the music would encourage young women to fall in love with them. If a Hopi child was naughty the mother could ask another woman to hold the child over a smoky juniper fire until the mother thought the young one had breathed enough smoke to cure the naughtiness. The Navajo dried the berries for necklaces and bracelets. Mothers put these "ghost beads" on their babies to prevent bad dreams.

Wild Gardening: The large junipers are excellent garden shrubs and trees, while low-growing junipers are good for borders and groundcovers. Most native junipers and horticultural varieties are drought tolerant. They are readily available from local nurseries and suitable for USDA zones 2 to 8.

Common Juniper berries
Juniperus communis

Rocky Mountain Juniper male cones
Juniperus scopulorum

Rocky Mountain Juniper berries
Juniperus scopulorum

Western Juniper berries
Juniperus occidentalis

DOGWOOD FAMILY   CORNACEAE

The dogwood family contains ten genera, including many species of perennial trees and shrubs. They are widely distributed, appearing in temperate zones on all continents except Australia. Dogwoods are ancient plants, some preserved as fossils in 50- to 60-million-year-old rocks from Eocene time. The leaves are usually opposite, simple, and entire with prominent veins. The flowers are borne singly or in branched clusters. They have four or five petals and an equal number of stamens. The fifty species in the *Cornus* genus are all native to the Northern Hemisphere.

Bunchberry   *Cornus canadensis*

Bunchberry grows only 2 to 8 inches tall. A few opposite leaves grow on the lower stem, but a whorl of four to six larger leaves forms near the top. They are elliptical, 1 to 3 inches long, and deeply veined. You will easily identify its single white "flower," typical of the dogwood family. Four bracts resembling white petals open above the whorl of leaves at the tip of each stem. The bracts surround the real flower—a dense cluster of tiny, purplish blossoms that bloom from May through July. Each one is less than a tenth of an inch across. As the season progresses, each minute flower produces a bright red, berrylike drupe with a hard, two-celled stone. The fruits grow in clusters, suggesting the name bunchberry.

This beautiful little plant stands out dramatically in shady wooded areas where it covers the ground. It thrives in meadows, woods, and bogs, from sea level to 8,000 feet and ranges from the Pacific Coast to the Atlantic. It grows in the coastal ranges of Alaska and British Columbia, south to Washington, Oregon, and northern California, and throughout the Rocky Mountains to New Mexico. It does not grow in Arizona.

Edibility: The scarlet fruits of bunchberry are edible raw as trail food but vary from fairly sweet to dry and tasteless. According to some Native Americans, they taste similar to salal. You can use them in puddings, jams, and sauces.

Historical Uses: Tribes of Washington's Olympic Peninsula differed in their opinions of bunchberries; the Makah ate the berries fresh, but the Quinault declared them poisonous. The Quileute used them in religious ceremonies.

Pioneers and Native Americans made a leaf tea that substituted for quinine, a bitter alkaloid derived from cinchona bark and used to treat malaria. The bunchberry leaf tea relieved coughs, fevers, kidney and lung ailments, and general aches and pains.

Modern herbalists find similar medicinal uses for bunchberry. An infusion of roots, leaves, and twigs is effective as an anti-inflammatory and a relief for fevers and headaches.

Wild Gardening: With white flowers and scarlet fruits, bunchberry is one of the showiest plants in the forest and a valuable clump-forming groundcover in shady gardens. Bunchberries grow in USDA zones 2 to 7 and are available from specialized nurseries.

Bunchberry flowers   *Cornus canadensis*

Bunchberry fruit   *Cornus canadensis*

Pacific Dogwood   *Cornus nuttallii*

Pacific dogwood is a 12- to 50-foot-tall, graceful tree. It has brownish black bark and leaves that are up to 5 inches long. They are elliptic to ovate, dark green above, paler beneath, and slightly hairy. In spring, tiny, greenish white blossoms form a cluster in the center of four to seven white or pinkish bracts that look like a large white flower. The white bracts contrast brilliantly with the green forest foliage. In early fall, the group of flowers becomes a cluster of tiny, red berries.

Pacific dogwood grows in mixed evergreen forests below 6,000 feet. It is common throughout the coastal ranges of California, Oregon, Washington, British Columbia, and northern Idaho. Lewis and Clark discovered Pacific dogwood at the mouth of the Sandy River in Multnomah County, Oregon, in 1805.

Edibility: Pacific dogwood berries are edible but hard, mealy, and often bitter. Try them only if you are desperately hungry.

Historical Uses: Native Americans sometimes stored whole berries for winter use, or more often, boiled fresh berries to make a refreshing juice, which they sweetened to taste. They made a tea from the bark for a tonic, laxative, or treatment for fever. Dogwood leaves were commonly dried and crushed for smoking, perhaps because they had a slight intoxicating effect. At least one tribe, the Quileute of Washington, used the berries of Pacific dogwood in their religious ceremonies.

Wild Gardening: Pacific dogwood is excellent for the home landscape and is readily available from nurseries. It grows best in the coastal environment in USDA zone 6. A large selection of other dogwood species and cultivars are suitable for USDA zones 3 to 8.

Pacific Dogwood flowers   *Cornus nuttallii*

Pacific Dogwood fruits with immature fruit cluster at left   *Cornus nuttallii*
—CHARLES WEBBER PHOTO, CALIFORNIA ACADEMY OF SCIENCE

Red Osier Dogwood   *Cornus sericea*

Until recently, red osier dogwood was called *Cornus stolonifera* in North America. Botanists now recognize it as the same species as the European plant, *C. sericea*.

The casual observer will not easily recognize this red-barked shrub as a relative of either bunchberry (*C. canadensis*) or Pacific dogwood (*C. nuttallii*). Red osier is a spreading bush, growing 3 to 15 feet tall with blazing red new growth. The lower branch tips often touch the ground and take root. Opposite leaves are 2 to 3 inches long, ovate, pointed at the tip, and fuzzy beneath. They have deep, parallel veins. Tiny, ¼-inch-wide, four-petaled, white flowers appear in flat-topped cymes that mature into small bunches of pea-size fruits. The berrylike drupes are bluish white and waxy.

Red osier prefers moist sites and typically forms streamside thickets. It grows from Alaska to southern California, on both sides of the Sierra Nevada, in the Great Basin, in the Rocky Mountains, and eastward to the Atlantic Coast.

Edibility: The bitter berries of red osier dogwood are edible but not palatable

Historical Uses: A few aboriginal groups throughout the West ate red osier berries in spite of the bitterness. For the Okanagan they were a staple food

Native Americans throughout the West made a decoction of plant roots and stems for medicinal purposes. This decoction was popular as an eye wash gynecological aid, "blood medicine" (tonic), cold and fever remedy, laxative and emetic. The Nespelem used the decoction to heal poison ivy rash and to eliminate thinning hair, itchy scalp, and dandruff. Many Native American dried the leaves and shredded bark and smoked the mixture, sometimes adding tobacco or kinnikinnick. For some groups, such as the Navajo and Blackfeet the smoking mix was a ceremonial aid.

Red osier wood is very hard, and natives carved implement handles, cooking tools, barbecue racks, discs for gambling games, and wooden bowls from it The Karok and Maidu of northern California twisted pliable branches and strips of shredded bark to make rope. Men of these tribes wore a small piece of the wood for a good luck charm. Many tribes used straight stems for arrows and slender, pliable stems for basketry.

Wild Gardening: Red osier dogwood is particularly desirable for landscaping in northern climates because the red stems stand out dramatically against the snow. It is hardy to USDA zone 3 and readily available from nurseries.

Red Osier Dogwood flowers   *Cornus sericea*

Red Osier Dogwood fruit   *Cornus sericea*

About two hundred species of trees and shrubs compose the elm family. The alternate, asymmetrical leaves have three main veins and are usually toothed. The stipules—leaflike appendages at the leaf bases—are paired. The inconspicuous male and female catkins, both on the same tree, emerge before the leaves. The blossoms have no petals or corolla, only greenish sepals and four to eight stamens. The one-seeded fruit is a drupe or a winged fruit.

Netleafed hackberry   *Celtis reticulata*

Netleafed hackberry has such tough wood that only the tiniest twigs are easily broken. The twigs are fuzzy, and the bark has warts and corky ridges. In spring, white partitions divide the hollow centers of the smaller twigs. The alternate, dark green deciduous leaves are 1 to 3 inches long and ovate to lance shaped, sometimes with teeth or lobes. The upper leaf surfaces are rough, and the undersides have a network of raised veins. They are asymmetrical at the base where the three main veins begin. The leaves are often infected with insect galls, and a fungus causes the twigs to form witches' brooms.

flowers

stem

Flowers near the top of the tree tend to be female, those near the bottom male, and those in the middle bisexual. The pistil of the female flower is split at the top, and the two parts extend in opposite directions. Together, they resemble a fuzzy, white worm. By September or October each female flower grows into a sweet orangish red to reddish black drupe with a large seed. The drupe hangs from the leaf axil by a ½-inch-long stalk and stays on the tree through winter.

Netleafed hackberry occupies dry slopes, ravines, rocky areas, river corridors, and canyons. It grows in eastern Washington, eastern Oregon, southern Idaho, southwestern Wyoming, Nevada, Utah, Colorado, Arizona, New Mexico, California, Texas, and Mexico. It is the most common tree in Hells Canyon on the Snake River between Idaho and Oregon, inhabiting ravines and terraces away from the river.

A similar species, **Palo blanco (C. *pallida*),** is a dense, spiny shrub of the desert with greenish yellow flowers and orange berries. It is only about 8 feet high. Its leaves are evergreen except in drought or unusual cold. They are 1 inch long, rough on both sides, and toothed only from the middle to the tip. Palo blanco grows in southern New Mexico, Arizona, Texas, and Mexico.

Edibility: You can eat the berries of netleafed hackberry either raw or dried. The large seeds are enclosed in thick, hard coats that must be removed prior to eating except when the dried berries are ground into flour. The berries get sweeter after the weather turns cold in fall.

Historical Uses: People have eaten hackberries for thousands of years. Archaeologists found hackberry seeds in the refuse heaps surrounding the sites of Java man (*Homo erectus*). In North America, the Navajo, Apache, and Dakota ate the berries, often grinding them first and shaping them into cakes. The Dakota used them primarily to season meat. The Navajo ate the sugary seeds and boiled the leaves and branches for a dark brown or red dye. Because the bark comes off in smooth slabs, the Pima and Papago of Arizona used it for sandals. The Tewa made handles for axes and hoes from the wood.

Wild Gardening: This small shade tree is well suited for gardens. Though drought tolerant, watering it well the first few years after planting encourages growth. It grows best in USDA zones 3 to 5.

Above: Netleafed Hackberry flowers *Celtis reticulata*

Top right: Netleafed Hackberry immature fruit with fuzzy pistil still attached *Celtis reticulata*

Bottom right: Netleafed Hackberry fruit *Celtis reticulata*

GINSENG FAMILY   ARALIACEAE

The large, palmately lobed or compound leaves of the ginseng family resemble hairy maple leaves. The fruits are like grapes but often have prickles. Small greenish flowers form umbels or racemes. They have five petals, and a fleshy disk covers the ovary. Flowers may be female, male, or bisexual. The fruit is a drupe. Roots of American ginseng (*Panax quinquefolius*), which is native to eastern North America, have been used as a tonic.

Sarsaparilla and Spikenards   *Aralia* species

The *Aralia* genus contains thirty aromatic herbs, shrubs, or small trees that grow in Asia, Malaysia, and North America. They have compound deciduous leaves, and the flowers are arranged in panicles.

Sarsaparilla (A. nudicaulis) is a shade-loving perennial with compound leaves, each of which has five oval to round leaflets. The 4-inch-long, evenly toothed leaflets taper to a sharp tip. Spherical umbels of greenish white flowers appear in May and June, hidden under the leaves. Dark purple to black berries are ¼ inch across with a single seed. Sarsaparilla is Spanish from *zarza*, meaning "bramble," and *parilla*, meaning "little vine," originally describing a tropical vine (*Smilax* species) that had a characteristic aroma. Early settlers in North America obtained a similar flavoring from A. *nudicaulis*, which they called sarsaparilla.

Sarsaparilla prefers moist, shady woods of the boreal, or northern coniferous, forest. It grows across Canada and from northeastern Washington to Montana, Colorado, and Michigan.

Elk clover (A. californica) grows 8 feet tall with 9-inch-wide leaves. The black berries contain poisonous seeds. It grows in California.

Spikenard (A. racemosa) has light green leaves up to 3 feet long with broad leaflets. The small, whitish flowers form in a branch of umbels that mature into purple berries. Spikenard grows in Utah, Arizona, and New Mexico.

Edibility: The berries of sarsaparilla are edible but not tasty. People made wine and beer from the berries and used the long, aromatic roots to flavor tea, mead, and root beer. The sarsaparilla used commercially to flavor beverages was obtained from either sarsaparilla roots or from the roots of the tropical vine of the genus *Smilax*.

The seeds of elk clover berries are **TOXIC**.

Historical Uses: Because sarsaparilla grows naturally only in the northern woods, Eastern and Canadian tribes used it more often than western tribes who had to travel far north to find it. The natives used it to make cough medicine. Eastern tribes boiled the roots of sarsaparilla and crushed them with those of sweet flag (*Acorus calamus*), another aromatic plant, to make a poultice for treating boils or pleurisy. In the Northwest, the Kwakuitl mixed sarsaparilla root with oil and took it for coughs and tuberculosis. Other tribes used sarsaparilla tea as a tonic and to get rid of pimples.

In 1623, the herbalist John Gerard said of sarsaparilla: "The roots are a remedie against long continual paine of the joynts and head, and against cold diseases." From 1880 to 1882, *United States Pharmacopoeia* listed sarsaparilla as a stimulant, a perspiration induSpikenardscer, a spring tonic, and an all-purpose medicine. The chemicals in *Aralia* species contain steroids that may increase the germ-killing activity of white blood cells.

Elk clover apparently has medicinal qualities, too. The Pomo and Mendocino used elk clover tea for treating colds and bronchitis and for washing sores.

Sarsaparilla fruit   *Aralia nudicaulis*
—MICHAEL GADOMSKI PHOTO,
PHOTO RESEARCHERS, INC.

Sarsaparilla flowers
Aralia nudicaulis

Devil's Club   *Oplopanax horridum*

Devil's club, a bad-smelling, deciduous shrub, grows from 1 to 3 feet tall. It may be erect but often spreads along the ground because its weak branches are soft and pithy inside. Many large, yellow spines stud the stems and undersides of the giant, maplelike leaves. If scratched by these spines, some people have an allergic reaction, and spines left in the skin may cause infection. The leaves have five to seven lobes, grow alternately on the stem, and are often 12 inches or more wide. The yellowish or greenish white flowers grow in dense, cone-shaped clusters at the branch tips. The prickly fruits are red, berrylike drupes.

Devil's club loves shade and prefers wet, well-drained sites in woods and along streams. It grows along the coast from Alaska to southern Oregon and east into Washington, northern Idaho, and western Montana. It also is present in Japan and the Great Lakes region.

Edibility: The acrid berries of devil's club are **TOXIC** for humans, but bears eat them.

Historical Uses: Devil's club was an important medicine for Native Americans. They used poultices of bark or leaves to treat arthritis, diabetes, fevers, coughs, tuberculosis, boils, and infections. Several northwestern groups cut off the thorns, peeled the bark away, and boiled the stems to make a decoction for treating arthritis and gonorrhea. The Crow smoked the root for headache. The Kwakuitl of British Columbia rubbed mashed berries into their scalps to get rid of lice. Modern herbalists use devil's club to stimulate respiration, as an expectorant for chest colds, and to treat adult-onset diabetes.

Northwest tribes believed devil's club kept evil spirits away, so they built lodges for their medicine men out of its wood and used its charcoal as protective face paint. The Nitinaht thought the paint gave them so much power no one could look them in the eye. The wood was also fashioned into fishing lures.

Wild Gardening: Devil's club would be a dramatic garden plant except its ferocious spines would discourage any nearby weeding. We found no source where it is available for purchase.

Devil's Club fruit
Oplopanax horridum

Devil's Club flowers
Oplopanax horridum

GOOSEBERRY FAMILY   GROSSULARIACEAE

Gooseberries are deciduous, often spiny shrubs with palmately lobed leaves that resemble maple leaves. The flowers are tubular or saucer shaped and attached above the ovary. They have five petals and five stamens. The fruit is a berry with several seeds and sometimes soft bristles.

Gooseberries and Currants   *Ribes* species

The *Ribes* genus includes gooseberries and currants. Gooseberries supposedly have spines and currants do not, but common names being inconsistent, a few "gooseberries" lack spines, and a few "currants" have them. All *Ribes* species have lobed, maplelike leaves but often with rounded points. The flowers usually have five stamens and five sepals fused into a tube or cup. The flower shape may be an adaptation to pollination by hummingbirds. Dried flowers stay attached to the berries forming little tails, the remnants of the sepals, on the end of the fruit.

The name *gooseberry* comes from the old English custom of stuffing roast goose with the berries. The name *currant* comes from Corinth, the home of a small purple grape (*Uva corinthiaca*), which is sold commercially as a currant.

sepal remnants

GOOSEBERRIES

Common gooseberry (R. inerme), a 7-foot-tall shrub, has 1- to 3½-inch long spines at the leaf nodes. The alternate leaves are toothed and have three to five deep lobes. Flower petals are green, sepals purplish, and stamens twice as long as the petals. The wine-colored berries lack prickles.

Common gooseberry forms thickets on open ridges. It grows from British Columbia south along the Cascade Range and Sierra Nevada, and south in the Rocky Mountains to New Mexico.

Sierra gooseberry (R. roezlii) is a 3-foot-tall, spiny shrub with tubular, purple and white flowers. The red to purple berries are spiny and fuzzy. It grows on dry slopes and open forests in most of the mountains of California and Oregon.

Swamp gooseberry (R. lacustre), also called black gooseberry or prickly currant, has three- to five-lobed leaves and smells mildly unpleasant. Golden prickles cover the shrub, and spines emerge at the leaf nodes. Avoid the spines as they can produce an allergic reaction. Swamp gooseberry usually grows 3 feet tall but can be prostrate and spreading. Its twigs are reddish brown. The small, reddish flowers are saucerlike and hang in drooping clusters. Bristles and gland-tipped hairs cover the dark purple berries. The many bristles prompted some British Columbia tribes to call this berry "hairy face."

Swamp gooseberry prefers wet places, particularly mountain meadows. It grows across the northern tier of western states as far south as Utah and Colorado.

continued on page 46

Sierra Gooseberry immature fruit   *Ribes roezlii*
Inset: Sierra Gooseberry fruit   *Ribes roezlii*

Swamp Gooseberry fruit
    Ribes lacustre

Swamp Gooseberry flowers
    Ribes lacustre

Gummy gooseberry (R. lobbii) has red flowers that look like fuchsias. The drooping flowers have red, recurving sepals with a central tube of mainly white petals and stamens that hang below them. The flowers resemble little dancers with slim torsos, slender legs, and tiny feet, all wearing split, rose-colored skirts over white skirts. Gummy gooseberry grows at mid-elevations along the Pacific Coast from Vancouver Island to northern California.

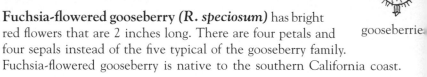

gooseberrie

Fuchsia-flowered gooseberry (R. speciosum) has bright red flowers that are 2 inches long. There are four petals and four sepals instead of the five typical of the gooseberry family. Fuchsia-flowered gooseberry is native to the southern California coast.

Mountain gooseberry (R. montigenum) is a spiny shrub with prickly, reddish berries. The whole plant is sticky, fuzzy, and bristly. Mountain gooseberry grows on dry, rocky slopes in the Sierra Nevada and Rocky Mountains.

Edibility: Gooseberries are edible and palatable. Cooking softens the bristles on the berries so they are not noticeable when eaten.

Florence's Gooseberry Catsup, page 200
Florence's Gooseberry-Currant Jam, page 194

Historical Uses: Native Americans ate all wild gooseberries when available, though they often did not gather large quantities. A few groups picked enough common gooseberry to mix with other berries to mash for dried cakes. The Okanagan mashed the berries and mixed them with bitterroot to trade with coastal people for salmon. Most Native Americans on the Northwest Coast ate swamp gooseberries fresh or cooked but took care not to be pricked by the spines as they caused an allergic reaction in some individuals.

Native Americans also used gooseberries medicinally. They created an infusion of gooseberry leaves and roots to treat sore throats, colds, fevers, tuberculosis, venereal disease, burns, wounds, and menstrual problems. The Skagit boiled the bark of swamp gooseberry to make a tea for childbirth. Native Americans disagreed over the effect of ingesting gooseberries on the digestive system. Some believed they were good for treating constipation; others used them to cure diarrhea.

Colonists used gooseberry juice to treat colds and sore throats. Contemporary herbalists think gooseberries and currants strengthen the immune system.

Fuchsia-Flowered Gooseberry flowers   *Ribes speciosum*

Fuchsia-Flowered
Gooseberry fruit
Ribes speciosum

CURRANTS

Wax currant (*Ribes cereum*), also called squaw currant, has grayish brown bark and alternate, fuzzy leaves with three to five lobes. The 1- to 2-inch-diameter, toothed leaves cluster at the ends of branches. White or pink, tubular flowers grow in short, drooping racemes. The flowers and fruit are sticky but not prickly.

currants

Wax currant grows on dry, rocky slopes to above timberline. It ranges from Saskatchewan west to British Columbia and from eastern Oregon's Blue Mountains south to California and east to the Rocky Mountains and Nebraska.

Golden currant (*R. aureum*) can grow to 10 feet tall. It has a spicy odor and no prickles. The 2-inch-diameter, lobed leaves are light green, not fuzzy, and kidney shaped with conspicuous veins. Six to nine bright yellow flowers cluster together in racemes. The color of the blossoms gives the plant its name, though they can be cream or red rather than golden. The fragrant flowers have a long, narrow flower tube that some insects have adapted to by boring a hole at its base to get at the nectar. The ⅜-inch-diameter berries are sweet and juicy and usually orangish red.

Golden currant grows from British Columbia east to Saskatchewan and south to California, Colorado, and Nebraska.

Sticky currant (*R. viscosissimum*) has fuzzy, sticky twigs and leaves. Hairs on both surfaces of the green leaves give them a grayish hue. Its greenish white to pinkish flowers are cylindrical, and its sticky, black berries are round to oval.

Sticky currant grows mainly on the eastern sides of the Cascade Range and British Columbia coast ranges and in the Sierra Nevada and Rocky Mountains.

Red-flowering currant (*R. sanguineum*) has trumpet-shaped, pale pink to bright red flowers that hang in drooping clusters in March and April. The shrub's crooked stems have reddish brown bark with no prickles. A waxy coating on the dark blue to black berries makes them look sky blue. This currant grows along the Pacific Coast as far south as northern California.

Stink currant (*R. bracteosum*) is covered with round yellow glands that make the plant smell like skunk or tomcat, particularly when crushed. The leaves are deeply lobed. Its white to greenish white flowers grow in 1-foot-long, erect clusters. The bluish black berries have a whitish bloom.

Stink currant grows from Alaska to northern California, mainly on the western side of the Cascade Range but occasionally as far east as the Okanogan Valley in central Washington.

Golden Currant fruit   *Ribes aureum*
Inset: Golden Currant flowers   *Ribes aureum*

Wax Currant flowers   *Ribes cereum*
Inset: Wax Currant fruit   *Ribes cereum*

Edibility: All currants are edible but some taste better than others. Wax currants are dry and seedy and have an odd, wild taste. If eaten in quantity they are emetic. They make good jelly, though it tastes better if flavored with a little apple juice or lemon juice. Golden currant has sweet, juicy berries. Sticky currant, red-flowering currant, and stink currant vary from insipid to downright bad.

 Grandma Hanford's Currant Cookies, page 185
Florence's Gooseberry-Currant Jam, page 194
Currant Granola, page 205

Historical Uses: Lewis and Clark discovered three species of currants—golden currant, wax currant, and sticky currant. At the Three Forks of the Missouri in July 1805, they saw Indians making pemmican from golden currants. Meriwether Lewis wrote in his journal, "This currant is really a charming fruit and I am confident would be preferred at our markets to any currant now cultivated in the U. States."

Other historical travelers found currants equally delightful. John Kirk Townsend's account of his journey across the Rocky Mountains with the Nathaniel Wyeth party in 1834 relates their joy in finding fresh currants. "In the mountain passes, we found an abundance of large yellow currants, rather acid, but exceedingly palatable to men who have been long living on animal food exclusively. We all ate heartily of them, indeed, some of our people became so much attached to the bushes, that we had considerable difficulty to induce them to travel again."

The Nez Perce and coastal Samish ate currants only when food was short. The Paiute ground dried currants, mixed them with flour from wild plant seeds, and cooked the mixture into porridge. California tribes used wax currants in pemmican and boiled the young leaves and twigs for a vegetable. They also ate the flowers. The Kwakuitl of British Columbia saved the currants for winter by boiling them in wooden boxes, adding powdered skunk cabbage leaves (*Lysichitum americanum*) as a preservative, and drying them in wooden frames. The dried berries were later soaked in water and mixed with the grease of the eulachon fish. They used special spoons fashioned from mountain goat horn to eat this festive dish. If a guest failed to finish the bowl of greased currants, he or she would have bad luck.

Native Americans made various decoctions of currants for ailments ranging from toothache to snakebite. The Kiowa of Montana made a leaf poultice for snakebites, and the Thompson of British Columbia washed their babies with a decoction of leaves and branches to make them strong. For eyewash, the Klallam of the Olympic Peninsula soaked currant bark in water and added human milk. The Navajo used a variety of wax currant as a guide for when to plant corn. As soon as the stems became green they ploughed, and as soon as the leaves emerged they planted.

Wild Gardening: Many *Ribes* shrubs, both gooseberries and currants, were dug up and burned from the 1930s to the 1950s as soon as it became known that the plants harbor the first stage of blister rust fungus. This fungus kills five-needled pines, particularly western and eastern white pine. It was accidentally imported to the United States from Europe about 1900. The eradication program did not work well, and currants are still plentiful, but some states prohibit the sale of bushes.

Top: Red-Flowering
Currant flowers   *Ribes Sanguineum*

Bottom: Red-Flowering
Currant fruit   *Ribes Sanguineum*

GRAPE FAMILY   VITACEAE

As many as five hundred species of grapes are widely distributed in tropical and temperate regions. The plants are deciduous, woody vines that climb by tendrils growing opposite the leaves. In arid regions they are almost erect shrubs. The leaves are simple rather than compound and palmately lobed. The tiny flowers, often unisexual, grow in narrow panicles. They have four to five petals with four to five stamens opposite them. Grapes are cultivated for their fruit and grown as screens and as ornamentals.

Grapes   *Vitis* species

The sixty-five species of *Vitis* grow in subtropical and temperate regions. These woody vines climb with tendrils that form opposite the leaf nodes and lack suction disks. There are male, female, and bisexual flowers, all greenish to yellowish. The fruit, either a rounded or egg-shaped grape, may have a whitish bloom.

California wild grape (*V. californica*), a woody vine that climbs by tendrils, resembles the cultivated grape, *V. vinifera*. The leaves of California wild grape are broadly heart shaped, often three lobed, and hairy on the undersurface. They have toothed margins. Small, greenish yellow flowers bloom in elongated clusters in spring from March to May or June, depending on the climate. Tiny, purple grapes with a dense, whitish bloom mature from midsummer to fall.

California wild grape grows along streambanks and canyons below 4,000 feet from southern Oregon through the foothills of the Cascade Range and Sierra Nevada to south-central California.

Desert grape (*V. girdiana*) differs from California wild grape in being a high climber and having young growth that appears white because it is covered with dense, woolly hairs. The ¼-inch-diameter berries are purplish black with little bloom.

Desert grape grows in canyon bottoms and along streams below 4,000 feet in oak woodlands and coastal sage scrub from southern California to Baja.

Edibility: All parts of a wild grape plant are edible—fruits, leaves, young shoots, and tendrils. The fruits are smaller, seedier, and less juicy than garden grapes and can be bitter.

 Wild Grape Jelly, page 197

Historical Uses: Indians ate wild grapes fresh, dried, and in juice. Grapes were not an important food for most native groups, but the leaves and vines were useful. Leaves were good for lining earth ovens, and when traveling, Indians chewed a handful of leaves to quench thirst. They used leaf poultices for snakebite and took leaf sap for diarrhea.

Native Americans used grape stems as rope, string, and twining material for baskets. With the rope and string, they tied bundles, moored canoes, or made fish traps. For ceremonies, berry juice was mixed with clay and used as a body paint for dancers.

Desert travelers still obtain water from grape vines. To obtain water, cut the vine near the ground and place it in a container. Then make a slantwise cut in the vine about 6 feet up that allows watery liquid to drip down the inner stem and into the container.

Wild California Grape fruit
Vitis californica

Below: Desert Grape fruit   *Vitis girdiana*
Inset: Desert Grape early spring growth covered with white woolly hairs   *Vitis girdiana*

Heath Family
ERICACEAE

The heath family contains about seventy genera and fifteen hundred species that are widely distributed in temperate climates around the world. The leaves are oval, simple, alternate, and smooth-edged. Some species have small flowers and others have large, spectacular flowers. They are bisexual and have eight or ten stamens. The genera in the western United States often have fused petals. The ovary is either above or below the single pistil. The flowers usually stay on the ends of the fruits as they ripen. The fruit is a drupe, a true berry, or a dry capsule that sometimes has a fleshy calyx.

Some of the most popular wild fruits and the choicest broadleafed evergreens for gardens are members of the heath family, including huckleberries, cranberries, manzanitas, wintergreens, rhododendrons, and azaleas.

Pacific Madrone   *Arbutus menziesii*

Pacific madrone is an evergreen tree with a wide crown that may grow 80 feet tall. The smooth bark peels, revealing a polished trunk with patches of green, brown, and red. Peeling reaches its height in July and August. On the lower trunks of old trees, the bark is reddish brown and fissured or divided into rectangular plates. The alternate, elliptical leaves are thick, shiny, and dark green. They are 2 to 5 inches long with small teeth and long leafstalks. Though the leaves are evergreen, they live only two years, turning red before they begin to fall in June of the second year.

Fragrant, ⅓-inch-long flowers appear in long, drooping clusters from March to early May. The flowers are jug shaped, white or pink, and attached by short stalks. From September to November, the berries turn red or bright orange, staying on the tree until birds eat them. The berries are ½ inch across, round to egg-shaped, with a warty surface and mealy texture.

Lewis and Clark noticed Pacific madrone at the Cascades of the Columbia River in the fall of 1805. Father Juan Crespi, the diarist for the Portola overland expedition of 1769, named the madrone tree. He called it *madroño*, which means "strawberry tree" in Spanish.

At higher elevations, Pacific madrone grows on upland, wooded slopes and at lower elevations it grows in canyons. It prefers moist coastal climates but tolerates moderate amounts of heat, cold, and drought. It grows along the Pacific Coast from southwestern British Columbia to southern California and in the central Sierra Nevada to 6,000 feet.

A similar species, **Arizona madrone (A. arizonica),** resembles Pacific madrone but grows half as tall. Its young bark is dark red, old bark is light gray, and twigs are red. Its leaves are lance-shaped, 3 inches long, and light green. Arizona madrone grows from 4,000 to 8,000 feet in southeastern Arizona, southwestern New Mexico, and Mexico.

Edibility: Madrone berries are edible raw, boiled, or steamed, but they taste bland, mealy, and sometimes bitter. Birds flock to them, but humans seldom do because eating more than a few causes stomach cramps. You can steep tea from the bark peels and serve it with a cinnamon stick.

Historical Uses: Native Americans used madrone in various ways. The Karok of California steamed the berries in a basket with madrone leaves on top, then dried and stored the berries. The Miwok only chewed the berries but didn't swallow them. Several groups dried and crushed the berries to make cider or to brew tea.

For colds and stomach ailments, the Pomo and Snohomish drank an infusion of madrone root, bark, and leaves. The Yuki used this treatment for sores and cuts and gave it to horses with sore backs. Modern herbalists use the leaves for bladder infections because, like other members of the heath family, madrone contains arbutin, the same substance as in cranberry juice.

Several coastal tribes used madrone wood for lodgepoles and for tools. Though madrone wood is an attractive reddish brown and fine grained, it is too brittle for commercial use. The Karok burned madrone in their ritual of First Salmon, but the Straits Salish never burned it because in their legend of the Great Flood, madrone wood anchored their canoe to the top of legendary Mount Newton.

The unusual peeling bark inspired some creative tales and uses. A Yurok legend explains how deer were created from a piece of madrone bark. In the mountains of northern California, Karok and Yurok children fashioned the bark into snow sleds, and Pomo children played with the leaves as paper dolls. Other groups sewed the inner bark together for dresses and made necklaces of the berries. They made a brown dye from the bark. The Straits Salish cooked pieces of madrone bark with the bulbs of camas (*Camassia quamash*) to color the bulbs pink.

Wild Gardening: The madrone is an attractive tree though the shedding bark, leaves, and twigs require some maintenance. It takes several years before a tree produces flowers and berries. Some cultivars are smaller and more compact than the native tree, making them suitable for the small garden. The berries attract birds. Madrones grow best in USDA zones 6 to 7.

c Madrone flowers   *Arbutus menziesii*   Pacific Madrone fruit   *Arbutus menziesii*

Manzanitas   *Arctostaphylos* **species**

All of the more than fifty species of *Arctostaphylos* are called manzanita except for kinnikinnick (*A. uva-ursi*) and bearberry (*A. alpina*). Most species in the genus have reddish brown, peeling bark; urn-shaped, white or pinkish flowers; applelike berries; and thick, leathery leaves. The name *manzanita* is Spanish, meaning "little apple."

Manzanitas have several unusual characteristics. One species; *A. glandulosa*, has a large, woody burl on its trunk at ground level and sprouts from its roots following fire—one of only a few manzanitas that do this. The seeds of many manzanitas will not germinate until heated by fire. Several manzanitas exhibit bark striping: strips of dead bark peel off, exposing strips of living bark. Growth is then restricted to branches and leaves connected to the living bark, creating a striped look, and as you might imagine, a crooked and gnarled shrub. Drought, fire, and shade cause bark striping.

In California, the many species of manzanita bloom from December through mid-June, varying in time by species and elevation. From May through October you can always find at least one species of manzanita with ripe berries.

Manzanitas sometimes hybridize with each other. For example, *Arctostaphylos* x *media* is a hybrid of kinnikinnick with hairy manzanita (*A. columbiana*).

Kinnikinnick (A. *uva-ursi*) has matlike foliage and reddish brown, peeling bark. Its shiny, dark green, leathery leaves are wider at the tip than at the base. Stomata are absent from the upper sides. In winter, the evergreen leaves become tinged with red or bronze. In spring, tiny, jug-shaped, white or pink flowers grow in short racemes at the tips of the branches. The ⅜-inch-diameter berries are bright red like miniature apples but are dry and seedy. The fruit ripen late and stay on the plants well into winter.

Kinnikinnick grows from the seacoast to alpine slopes in open places in dry woods, in chaparral, or at the edges of forests. The most widespread of the manzanitas, it ranges from Eurasia across Canada and the northern part of the United States and as far south as northern California, New Mexico, and Virginia.

Pinemat manzanita (A. *nevadensis*) resembles kinnikinnick but has pointed leaves and reddish brown berries. Because it usually grows at high elevations, its leaves lie mainly parallel to the ground to absorb more of the sun's heat than they would if they were vertical. It blooms in June.

Pinemat manzanita inhabits moist places or dry, rocky slopes in the woods, usually at 5,000 to 10,000 feet elevation, though sometimes as low as 2,000 feet. It grows in the Sierra Nevada, in the coast ranges from northern California to Washington, and in mountain ranges in Nevada.

Greenleaf manzanita (A. *patula*) is a spreading, much-branched shrub that grows 3 to 6 feet tall. Its several stems grow from an enlarged burl, an overgrowth of wood and bark that forms a big lump at the base of the plant. The smooth bark is reddish brown. The broadly ovate to almost round leaves are

Kinnikinnick berries   *Arctostaphylos uva-ursi*

Pinemat Manzanita berries
Arctostaphylos nevadensis

Kinnikinnick flowers
Arctostaphylos uva-ursi

bright green or yellowish green and about 1¼ inches long. No other manzanita has bright green leaves. Some leaves grow vertically to deflect the sun's rays and keep the plant cool at warm sites. Its berries are dark brown. It is the most common manzanita in the Great Basin and spreads easily where snow weighs down the branches, which grow roots where they touch the ground.

Greenleaf manzanita prefers open ponderosa pine (*Pinus ponderosa*) and red fir (*Abies magnifica*) forests at elevations of 2,000 to 9,000 feet. It grows in the Sierra Nevada, the northern California coastal ranges north to Oregon, and in Nevada and Utah.

Bigberry manzanita (A. glauca) is an evergreen shrub reaching a height of 12 feet, with smooth, reddish brown bark. Its leaves are grayish green, elliptic to ovate and up to 1¼ inches across. Pink to white flowers produce a round, sticky, brownish berry about ¾ inch in diameter.

Bigberry manzanita is common on dry slopes below 4,500 feet. It inhabits chaparral communities and Joshua tree (*Yucca brevifolia*) woodlands in the coastal ranges of southern California and Baja.

Edibility: Kinnikinnick berries tend to be dry and sometimes astringent, and berries of other manzanitas are usually mealy and insipid. However, pioneers and Native Americans used them in beverages, jellies, pies, cobblers, and sometimes wine. Kinnikinnick leaves can be **TOXIC** so medicinal tea made with the leaves should not be used for more than a couple of days.

Historical Uses: The abundant kinnikinnick berries were an important food source for some California natives, but in the Northwest, most Native Americans ate kinnikinnick berries only in times of food scarcity. They apparently found them, as Meriwether Lewis wrote in his journal, "very tasteless and insipid." Arctic tribes and those of coastal British Columbia and Washington usually soaked kinnikinnick berries in water or grease to reduce the dryness. Some groups preserved the berries in oil. The Kootenay of northern Idaho cooked them like popcorn in an oil-covered pan.

Manzanita berries of many species were a staple food for the Cahuilla. They often divided the berry slopes among families so that each family "owned" a patch. They ate large quantities of berries, either raw or dried, and if the berries were bitter, they added wild honey for sweetening. They often pulverized dried berries and mixed them into acorn soup or with other fruits. The Miwok mixed them with salmon eggs and cooked the mixture in a basket with hot rocks.

Native Americans of the Northwest dried the leaves of kinnikinnick for smoking by toasting them beside a fire. Because kinnikinnick leaves don't burn easily in a pipe, they were often mixed with other more flammable leaves such as willow and red osier dogwood. Once tobacco was available, the smoker added it to kinnikinnick.

Throughout the West, tribes formulated medicines from manzanitas. A decoction of leaves was used for an antiseptic wash to treat poison oak rash and was taken to cure headaches, coughs, colds, and cuts. Dried kinnikinnick leaves were powdered and sprinkled on burns. To cure earache, the Flathead blew kinnikinnick smoke into the aching ear. For coughs and colds, the Cheyenne drank tea made from the leaves and ate the berries. They also burned the leaves to drive away evil spirits from people considered insane. The Blackfeet compounded a salve of grease, hooves, and boiled kinnikinnick to cure rashes, sores, and itching scalp. Several tribes made infusions of the leaves for kidney disease, urinary infections, and diabetes.

Early herbalists used kinnikinnick for treating gonorrhea and as an astringent, tonic, and diuretic. The Roman physician Galen said kinnikinnick was good for "hot burnings and cholericky agues." From 1820 to 1936, the *United States Pharmacopoeia* listed it as an approved medicine. Kinnikinnick contains arbutin, which reacts with chemicals in the urine to produce hydroquinone, a germicide that helps kill bacteria. Some peoples' urine turns green after eating the berries. Today, kinnikinnick tea, also called bearberry tea, is sold for bladder and kidney problems.

Native Americans carved tools, utensils, and tobacco pipes out of manzanita wood. They cherished the beautiful grain of burls that grow at the base of some manzanitas. The Hupa carved 4-inch-long pipes for everyday use and 12-inch-long ones for ceremonies.

Wild Gardening: Kinnikinnick is an excellent groundcover, particularly for dry sites and steep slopes. The berries attract small wildlife and birds to the yard. Manzanitas range widely and grow in USDA zones 2 to 8.

Greenleaf
Manzanita flowers
Arctostaphylos patula

Wintergreens *Gaultheria* species

The heath family includes two genera with species called wintergreen: *Pyrola* and *Gaultheria*. We only discuss species of the *Gaultheria* because they produce fleshy fruits. *Pyrola* species produce dry capsules. *Gaultheria* species are erect to prostrate shrubs that usually spread by underground stems called rhizomes. Urn- or bell-shaped, white flowers contrast with leathery, evergreen leaves. The fruit is dry, has many seeds, and is covered by a fleshy calyx. Salal (*G. shallon*), an important food for Native Americans, is discussed separately on pages 62–63.

Alpine wintergreen (*G. humifusa*), a creeping, evergreen shrub, forms mats·less than 5 inches high. Its alternate leaves are rounded to oval, about ½ inch long, with smooth or toothed margins. Tiny urn-shaped flowers, ¼ inch in diameter, grow singly in the leaf axils in July and August. The ¼-inch-diameter berries are red.

Alpine wintergreen prefers mossy banks or moist, subalpine and alpine slopes in open areas or coniferous forests. It grows from British Columbia south to California and in the Rocky Mountains as far south as Colorado.

Slender wintergreen (*G. ovatifolia*) has sprawling stems, hairy twigs and sepals, and 2-inch-long leaves. Its flowers are white bells, and its berries are bright red. It grows in British Columbia south to Idaho and through the Cascade Range to northern California.

Creeping snowberry (*G. hispidula*) has white berries, reddish stems, and hairs on the undersides of its leaves. Creeping snowberry is a plant of interior British Columbia, northern Idaho, and northeastern Washington.

Edibility: Wintergreen berries are edible and flavorful. Oil of wintergreen, obtained from the leaves, is **TOXIC** in all but minute quantities so we do not recommend leaf tea. Chemicals in wintergreen oil are closely related to those in aspirin so people allergic to aspirin should avoid both the leaves and the berries, which also contain small amounts of the oil.

Historical Uses: Native Americans occasionally used wintergreen berries for food. The Hoh of the Olympic Peninsula ate the berries of slender wintergreen, using them fresh and also in jelly. The Quileute used them for sauce.

Several western tribes made tea from wintergreen leaves to cure fevers, rheumatism, and upset stomach. They also chewed the leaves to sweeten the breath. Settlers used wintergreen berries to treat scurvy. Today, wintergreen is used in rubs for aches and pains as it causes increased blood flow, which seems to warm the skin and counteract pain. It is also a popular flavoring for candies and perfume.

Wild Gardening: G. *procumbens*, the original source of wintergreen flavoring and a native to the eastern United States, is a groundcover and grows in USDA zone 4.

Creeping Snowberry fruit   *Gaultheria hispidula*
—JOHN KALLAS PHOTO, WILD FOOD ADVENTURES

Salal   *Gaultheria shallon*

Salal, a spreading shrub that grows 6 or more feet tall, forms thickets. Its leathery, 2- to 4-inch-long leaves are dark green on top and lighter underneath with prominent veins. The leaves are ovate to elliptic, broadest at the base, and finely toothed. Racemes of hairy, sticky flowers hang from the ends of the branches, blooming from March through June. Seedy, ½-inch-diameter, red to black berries ripen from August to October. Seeds often germinate on fallen logs. On a western journey, 1823–1827, Scottish botanist David Douglas wrote in his journal, "In my walks I have frequently seen the young plants on the stumps of trees 4 to 10 feet from the ground and on dead wood growing luxuriantly."

Salal likes moist to dry woods from low to medium elevations. It grows from the eastern base of the Cascade Range to the Pacific Coast. It is common in coastal areas from southern California to Washington, Oregon, and British Columbia.

Edibility: Salal berries are edible and can be juicy or bland. Some people say they taste a little like almond-flavored blueberries.

Salal-Pear Sauce, page 202
Salal Relish à la Pobanz, page 202

Historical Uses: Salal berries were a staple food of tribes in the Northwest and California. The Quileute dipped a whole twig with berries on it in whale oil and ate them off the twig. Others mashed the berries and dried them in cakes or loaves that weighed as much as 15 pounds. Before eating the cakes they soaked them in water and dipped them in whale or seal oil. Coastal tribes such as the Haida of British Columbia stored the cakes in cedar boxes. When they ate the dried berries, they mixed them with the grease of a small fish called eulachon and ate them with special black spoons carved from mountain goat horn.

Salal leaves have medicinal value. The Klallam, Bella Coola, and Quileute of the Northwest chewed the leaves and spit them on burns and sores. Others chewed the leaves as a remedy for thirst and hunger pangs. A decoction of leaves was commonly prepared for coughs, diarrhea, and tuberculosis. Modern herbalists use salal much as the Native Americans once did, using a decoction of leaves for coughs, diarrhea, and urethritis, and a poultice for abrasions.

Employees of the Hudson Bay Company at Fort Vancouver made wine out of salal. David Douglas collected salal seeds and brought them to Britain in 1828.

Wild Gardening: Salal, a spreading shrub, is most suited to gardens west of the Cascade Range and Sierra Nevada. It grows best under open stands of ever greens, but it will form a thicket in sunny spots if the soil drainage is good. Salal is available from specialized nurseries and grows in USDA zones 6 and 7.

Salal flowers   *Gaultheria shallon*

Salal berries   *Gaultheria shallon*

Blueberries
Huckleberries   *Vaccinium* species

In the genus *Vaccinium*, botanists do not formally distinguish between blue-berries and huckleberries. Plants with strong-flavored, black or purplish berries are usually called huckleberries. However, some berries called huckleberries in the eastern United States are in their own genus, *Gaylussacia*, and have fewer and larger seeds than those of *Vaccinium* species. *Huckleberry* is an American corruption of the British *whortleberry*, which came from the Anglo Saxon *wyrtil*, meaning "little shrub," and *beri*, meaning "berry." All *Vaccinium* species have a crown made of the leftover flower on the end of the berry opposite its stem. In some blueberries, this crown is a cylindrical pit.

To further confuse things, a shrub of a different genus, *Menziesia ferruginea*, is called fool's huckleberry. The ⅜-inch-long flowers are pink or reddish yellow and urn shaped like those of the huckleberries. All parts of the plant are poisonous, but its "berries" are not part of the plant. Instead, the fungus *Exobasidium vaccinii* pro-duces pink, berrylike structures on the undersides of the leaves. Some tribes of the Northwest Coast ate the fungus berries, which apparently are not poisonous. The Tsimshian of coastal British Columbia ate the fungus even though they believed they were the snot of Henaaksiala, a mythical being who stole corpses.

calyx remnant

We have included the most common huckleberries and blueberries below. For information on other western species, consult a detailed flora such as *The Jepson Manual: Higher Plants of California* edited by James C. Hickman and *Flora of the Pacific Northwest* by C. L. Hitchcock and A. Cronquist.

Evergreen huckleberry (V. *ovatum*), also called California huckleberry, has shiny, toothed leaves and shiny, black berries with no bloom. The ever-green leaves are elliptic and leathery, and the center vein is in a deep groove. From March to May, white or pink, bell-shaped flowers grow in racemes surrounded by short, red bracts. The berries ripen in late October or early November and stay on the bushes over winter.

Evergreen huckleberry grows along the Pacific Coast from British Columbia to California.

Mountain huckleberry (V. *membranaceum*) grows 6 feet tall and has alternate, bright green leaves and urn-shaped, pink to pale yellow flowers. Its berries are reddish purple to black, usually without a bloom. The 3-inch-long leaves are elliptical, sawtoothed, and sharp-pointed. They turn reddish orange in autumn. Twigs are yellowish green, and the bark is gray and shredded. The ¼- to ½-inch-long flowers form in the leaf axils on long stalks. At the end of the ⅓-inch-diameter berries is a deep pit. The berries are tart but among the most delicious of the huckleberries.

   continued on page 66

Evergreen Huckleberry flowers and
immature fruits   *Vaccinium ovatum*

vergreen Huckleberry fruit
Vaccinium ovatum

Mountain huckleberry grows at middle to subalpine elevations in woods, wet meadows, and mountain clearings. It is particularly common on slopes that have burned. It ranges from Alaska south to the Oregon-California border and east to Idaho, Montana, Wyoming, and Michigan.

Western huckleberry (V. occidentale) has fuzzy, narrow leaves that are whitish green, toothless, and broadest toward the tip. The flowers, solitary or paired, are the typical little white or pinkish jugs or urns of the *Vaccinium* genus. The ¼-inch-diameter blue to blackish berries have a whitish bloom and are sweet but not as tasty as those of some other species.

Western huckleberry grows in wet places in meadows and rocky ridges and along streams and lake margins from British Columbia south along the eastern slopes of the Cascade Range and Sierra Nevada. It also inhabits the Rocky Mountains south to Montana, Utah, and Nevada.

Grouse whortleberry (V. scoparium), also called littleleaf huckleberry, is a low, creeping shrub with ½-inch-long, pale green leaves and squarish, pale green branches. The leaves are finely toothed. The tiny, light red berries smell like huckleberry jam when ripe. The ⅛-inch-long flowers are pink, solitar , and urn shaped. Stems are so close together that after the leaves turn yellow and fall, the plants could be used for brooms.

Grouse whortleberry grows in Canada and across the West as far south as Utah and Colorado. It is most common in the Rocky Mountains where it often is the only plant under lodgepole pine *(Pinus contorta).*

Oval-leafed blueberry (V. ovalifolium) has grooved, yellowish green to reddish branches. The thin, pale green leaves have rounded ends and no teeth. Solitary, pink flowers appear before the leaves and are so narrow at the outer end they look like little globes. The purplish black berries have so much bloom they look gray or pale blue. The berries, which ripen as early as July, have bigger seeds than other blueberries and rot easily.

Oval-leafed blueberry prefers bogs and forests from Alaska to Oregon and east to Idaho, Montana, Michigan, and Quebec. Large concentrations of it grow along the Pacific Coast.

Cascade huckleberry (V. deliciosum) has rose-colored flowers, blue juicy berries, and leaves that turn bright red in autumn. It is a low, spreading shrub that often dominates entire slopes in the Cascade Range from northern Oregon to British Columbia and in the Olympic Mountains.

Alaskan blueberry (V. alaskaense) has bronze-colored flowers, yellowish green twigs, and purple berries with a blue bloom. The main leaf vein is hairy underneath. It grows in the Cascade Range and in the coast ranges from Alaska to northwestern Oregon.

continued on page 68

Grouse Whortleberry fruit
Vaccinium scoparium

Western Huckleberry flowers
Vaccinium occidentale

Western Huckleberry fruit   *Vaccinium occidentale*
Inset: Unripe Western Huckleberry fruit   *Vaccinium occidentale*

Red huckleberry (*V. parvifolium*) has light green leaves, green branches, and bright pink to reddish orange berries. Young leaves stay on the plant over winter. The greenish white to pinkish yellow flowers bloom in April and May. The ½-inch-diameter berries, which ripen in August and September, taste tart and flavorful.

Red huckleberry grows in coastal forests from Washington to Alaska.

Edibility: Blueberries and huckleberries are aromatic and delicious. Those with the more tart flavor are usually called huckleberries. Coastal Indians picked evergreen huckleberries as late as December, believing they tasted better after the first frost.

Blueberry Muffins, page 179
Nancy's Strawberry-Blueberry Muffins, page 180
Blueberry Molasses Cake, page 183
Huckleberry Pie, page 186
Huckleberry Bread Pudding, page 188
Huckleberry Jam, page 195
Lavendar Blueberry Jello, page 197
Mixed Fruit Compote, page 198
Huckleberry Sauce, page 201

Historical Uses: Northwest tribes used special combs made of wood or salmon backbones to strip huckleberries and blueberries off the bushes. They dried the berries in the sun or by smoking, squashed them into cakes, and wrapped them in leaves or bark for storage. A British Columbia tribe kept their berry cakes rolled on sticks.

Robert Brown, in his 1868 paper on wild foods of the Northwest tribes, wrote that all around the Indian villages vast quantities of huckleberries formed into cakes would be drying on roofs and platforms "supervised by some ancient hag, whose hands and arms are dyed pink with them." Women or their families often "owned" the berry grounds. All the fields were named, and well-worn trails connected them.

For the Nez Perce and Chinook, September was berry month, the time of one of the four seasonal first fruits celebrations. After the ceremony, the Indians left for the berry-picking grounds to stay until mid-October. The tribe had a great time on these expeditions, and early missionaries didn't appreciate this at all. Henry Brewer of the Mount Adams Mission in Washington wrote, "The absence of our Indian converts so long a time during the berry season

Red Huckleberry fruit
Vaccinium parvifolium

being surrounded as they are by every possible bad example, and separated from the watchful care of their teachers, in many cases proves very injurious to their piety."

Native Americans used huckleberries and blueberries as medicines. They gave blueberry tea to women in labor and used the juice of red huckleberry to control excessive menstruation. The Makah gave an infusion of evergreen huckleberry to women after childbirth to help them regain their strength.

Many widely scattered native groups made infusions from bark, leaves, roots, or stems and used the liquid as an all-purpose medicine to stimulate appetite and to treat arthritis, heart trouble, diabetes, colds, and nausea.

Wild Gardening: Because of their edible berries and attractive foliage, blueberries and huckleberries are splendid shrubs for the garden. Evergreen huckleberry, often used as greenery by florists, is a particularly desirable ornamental. Specialized nurseries offer a wide choice of natives and cultivars that grow in environments ranging from USDA zones 3 to 6. *Vaccinium* species prefer acidic soil.

Cranberries   *Vaccinium* species

Cranberries are in the same genus as huckleberries and blueberries, but we treat them separately because of their tartness. Their flavor resembles that of V. *macrocarpon*, the cranberry native to the northeastern United States that is harvested commercially. The plants called highbush cranberries are in the honeysuckle family and discussed on page 84.

Bog cranberry (V. *oxycoccus*) is a spreading, woody shrub with dark, evergreen, egg-shaped leaves that are less than ½ inch long. The pointed leaves have rolled edges and a thick, whitish coat of wax on the undersides. The four-petaled white or pink flowers grow from the leaf axils near the ends of the branches, alone or in nodding clusters. The petals are bent back. Like all *Vaccinium* species, there are twice as many stamens as petals. The ½-inch-diameter berries are at first green and covered with tiny dots. They turn red at the first frost.

This cranberry grows only in sphagnum moss, putting down roots from the leaf nodes. Mycorrhizae, threadlike fungi that act as extra root hairs, are associated with this species as well as other *Vaccinium*. The fungi increase the uptake of nitrogen and phosphorus, nutrients that are scarce in the acidic soil of sphagnum bogs.

Bog cranberry grows in northern latitudes around the world in bogs, forests, and muskegs, always associated with sphagnum moss. In the western United States it inhabits western Washington, western Oregon, and northern Idaho.

Lowbush cranberry (V. *vitis-idaea*), also called lingonberry, is a distinctive mat-forming, evergreen shrub with alternate, leathery leaves that are usually less than ½ inch long. A prominent midvein marks the upper side of the leaf and glandular hairs coat the underside. Its berries are bright red and shiny.

Lowbush cranberry grows along the coasts of British Columbia and Alaska and in New England.

Edibility: Cranberries are thin-skinned, juicy, and edible. Bog cranberries taste like those grown commercially. Cooking reduces the tartness.

Lowbush Cranberry Coffee Cake, *page 181*
Lowbush Cranberry Cake, *page 184*
Saucy Cranberry-Elderberry Chicken, *page 190*
Lowbush Cranberry Stuffing, *page 191*

Historical Uses: Bog cranberries and lowbush cranberries were important foods for Native Americans when available. Natives usually boiled the cranberries and stored them in oil. In winter they served the berries whipped with snow and mixed with the grease of the tiny eulachon fish. Fresh berries helped quench thirst. In Washington, the Quinault, Klallam, and Makah picked bog cranberries when they were green and steamed them, or stored them in moss until they were soft and brown.

Cranberry juice has been a cure for bladder infection since early times. The chemical arbutin in cranberries prevents bacteria from adhering to the bladder wall. However, if an infection is already present, the juice may irritate the bladder.

Bog Cranberry fruit   *Vaccinium oxycoccus*
—BOB MOSELEY PHOTO

HOLLY FAMILY　　　　　　　　AQUIFOLIACEAE

Most of the four hundred species of holly are in a single genus, *Ilex*, and grow in the tropics.

Hollies　　　　　　　　　　　　*Ilex* species

Hollies have simple, alternate, evergreen, leathery leaves. The flowers are white or green, and the berries are red, yellow, or black. Male and female flowers, usually on separate plants, are small and clustered along the twigs. There are four petals and four sepals, which remain on the fruit. The fruit has four hard stones.

English holly (*I. aquifolium*), introduced from Eurasia, is common in western gardens and parks. We included it because its berries are poisonous. It has glossy, evergreen leaves with large, spiny teeth. The ⅜-inch-diameter shiny, red berries stay on the tree over winter. In May, racemes of white, bell-shaped flowers with four rounded petals perfume gardens. Only the female trees have berries.

English holly grows best in cool, wooded areas and is often cultivated in the mild climate west of the Cascade Range.

Yaupon holly (*I. vomitoria*), a native species, has toothed leaves without the spines characteristic of English holly. It has shiny red or yellow berries. Yaupon holly grows in New Mexico, Texas, and in the southeastern United States from Virginia to Florida.

Edibility: The berries of all hollies are **TOXIC** and trigger violent vomiting if consumed. The leaves are nontoxic.

Historical Uses: The Cherokee used yaupon berries as an emetic to produce visions and as a remedy for kidney disease. They also chewed its berries for indigestion. Several tribes made tea from the leaves, which contain caffeine and can also be emetic. Spanish explorers steeped the leaves for tea as early as 1542.

Wild Gardening: Hollies are elegant garden plants, and you can choose from dozens of varieties. Hollies are generally hardy in USDA zone 6 though a few species are hardy to zone 4. Buy two plants, one male and one female, to produce berries.

English Holly berries   *Ilex aquifolium*

HONEYSUCKLE FAMILY   CAPRIFOLIACEAE

Most species in the honeysuckle family are woody vines and shrubs. The leaves are opposite and simple except for genera such as elderberry (*Sambucus* species), which has compound leaves with opposite leaflets. The flowers are usually arranged in branched clusters. The sometimes showy flowers are more often small and bisexual with a minute calyx and tubular corolla of four or five lobes. The family includes such diverse relatives as elderberry, twinberry, snowberry, and highbush cranberry.

Twinberries
Honeysuckles   *Lonicera* species

Of the more than two hundred species worldwide, about twenty-five *Lonicera* species are native to North America, many of them cultivated. One or two pairs of leaves are often fused around the stem just below the spikes or pairs of tubular flowers. The fruit is a berry.

Black twinberry (*L. involucrata*) is a 10-foot-tall deciduous shrub with brown or purplish peeling bark. Its opposite, 5-inch-long, lance-shaped to oblong leaves are dark green and woolly beneath. Sticky, yellow flowers grow in pairs at the base of the leaves during late June and July. They are 1/2 inch long, tubular, and flaring. Crimson, cup-shaped bracts surround each pair of shiny black berries.

Lewis and Clark discovered black twinberry as they traveled along the Columbia River in September 1805. Black twinberry grows all across western North America as far south as Arizona and as far east as Quebec. This wide spread shrub prefers moist, shady places such as streamsides and canyon bottoms.

Red twinberry (*L. utahensis*), also called Utah honeysuckle, has red berries but lacks the red bracts of black twinberry. Red twinberry grows at middle and high elevations in the mountains from British Columbia and Alberta south to California, Utah, and Wyoming.

Chaparral honeysuckle (*L. interrupta*) is a shrub with a rigid trunk and climbing or sprawling branches. Its evergreen leaves are elliptic and about inches long. When young, the branches and leaves are purple and dusted with a white bloom. The flowers are yellow and the berries red. Chaparral honeysuckle occupies moist, shaded slopes along the Pacific Coast from British Columbia to southern California.

California honeysuckle (*L. hispidula*) trails or climbs, but the stems do not have clinging tendrils. The flowers are pink or purplish and the berries red. California honeysuckle grows along streams and on wooded slopes below 2,500 feet in the Sierra Nevada and west of the Cascade Range.

continued on page 7

Black Twinberry fruit   *Lonicera involucrata*

Red Twinberry flowers   *Lonicera utahensis*

Northwest honeysuckle (*L. ciliosa*), also called orange honeysuckle, is usually a climbing vine with twining stems. Its 3-inch-long leaves are ovate with hairy margins and undersides. The upper leaves encircle the stem to make a cup for the orange, tubular flowers and for the ¼-inch-diameter, red berries. Lewis and Clark found it along the Lolo Trail in northern Idaho in June 1806. It is widespread in the Northwest from northern California to British Columbia, Idaho, and Montana. It also grows in Arizona.

Double honeysuckle (*L. conjugialis*) has two berries that fuse as they ripen. It has dark purple flowers, 2- to 3-inch-long leaves, and tiny bracts around the flowers and berries. It grows on wooded slopes from 4,000 to 10,000 feet elevation in the Sierra Nevada, on the western side of the Cascade Range, and in western Nevada.

Northwest Honeysuck

Edibility: Most honeysuckle berries are inedible and **TOXIC**. You should not eat them, and most taste bad anyway. The bitter, horrible taste of black twinberry lingers for hours.

Historical Uses: Most Native Americans did not eat honeysuckle berries though children often sucked sweet nectar from the flowers of orange honeysuckle. They named the bitter berries of black twinberry "raven's food" and "monster's food," and some believed if they ate the berries they would be unable to speak. A few California tribes like the Maidu and Modoc ate the berries

Western tribes had a multitude of medicinal uses for twinberries and honeysuckles. An infusion made from bark or berries was commonly used for colds, sore throats, skin infections, and for dressing wounds and burns. The Swinomish of Washington bathed young girls in the tea to make their hair long and shiny. They also crushed leaves to put on the breasts of nursing mothers to stimulate milk production. Chehalis women drank an infusion of leaves as a contraceptive, but the Thompson women thought it had the opposite effect—they drank the tea to help them become pregnant. The Nitinaht of Vancouver Island rubbed the bark on their bodies as a relief for nervous breakdown.

Native Americans used the twining stems for basketry, weaving, and lashing, and they used the berries for making purple and black paint. Hollow stems of orange honeysuckle were used for pipe stems. Navajo hunters chewed the leaves and spit them on their weapons for good luck.

Wild Gardening: Popular ornamental plants, honeysuckles are intensely fragrant and have showy yellow or red blossoms. The sweet nectar entices hummingbirds and bees to the garden. The red berries cling to the vine throughout much of winter. Many species and cultivars are available from nurseries and grow in a variety of climates in USDA zones 3 to 7.

Northwest Honeysuckle flower   *Lonicera ciliosa*

Northwest Honeysuckle berries   *Lonicera ciliosa*

Elderberries   *Sambucus* **species**

Elderberries—whose pithy stems could be fashioned into musical instruments—received the genus name *Sambucus* from the Greek stringed instrument *sambuca*, which was made of alder wood. Elderberries are large deciduous shrubs or small trees that lack a main trunk and have serrated, pinnately compound leaves. White or cream-colored flowers appear in panicles at the ends of branches and mature into tiny drupes. All plant parts are toxic except for the cooked fruit. The twenty *Sambucus* species are native to temperate and subtropical regions.

Blue elderberry (*S. cerulea*) is a large shrub or small tree that grows from 6 to 20 feet tall, with brittle, pith-filled branches and grayish brown bark. You'll readily recognize its lush, green foliage. Each pinnately compound leaf has five to nine lance-shaped leaflets, 3 to 6 inches long and finely toothed. Small, creamy white flowers bloom in large, flat-topped clusters—a conspicuous display in May and June. Bunches of dark blue berries covered with a whitish bloom mature in August and September. The species name, *cerulea*, is from the Latin *caeruleus*, meaning "sky blue."

Blue elderberry prefers low to middle elevations in coniferous forests. It grows throughout California, the coastal ranges of Oregon, Washington, and British Columbia, east to the Rocky Mountains, and south to Arizona and New Mexico. Lewis and Clark collected blue elderberry as they traveled across Oregon in 1805, and Lewis described it during the winter of 1806 when camped at Fort Clatsop.

Red elderberry (*S. racemosa*) resembles blue elderberry, but its compound leaves usually have five to seven leaflets and its creamy white flowers bloom in a rounded or pyramidal cluster. The cluster becomes a spectacular bunch of shiny, red berries in fall.

Red elderberry is common in damp coastal woods, subalpine meadows and open forests from sea level to mid-elevations. It grows throughout the coastal ranges from Alaska to California.

Desert elderberry (*S. mexicana*) resembles blue elderberry, but both its leaflets and inflorescences are smaller. The berries can be either blue or white and have a white bloom.

Desert elderberry is a tree of the southwestern deserts. It grows along streambanks and in open woodlands below 4,500 feet from southern California to Baja, in pinyon-juniper woodlands of the Mojave Desert, and in Arizona.

Edibility: All blue elderberries are edible and rich in vitamin A, calcium, thiamin, and niacin. Only berries and blossoms should be consumed because the stems, leaves, and bark may be **TOXIC**. Red elderberries are not recommended, though Native Americans ate them after cooking. The hydrocyanic acid content can cause severe intestinal upset if eaten raw.

continued on page 80

Blue Elderberry flowers   *Sambucus cerulea*

Blue Elderberry flowers   *Sambucus cerulea*

Elderflower Tea, page 178
Saucy Cranberry-Elderberry Chicken, page 190
Elderberry Jelly, page 194
Mixed Berry Syrup, page 203
Lotion for Chapped Hands, page 207

Historical Uses: Elderberries were important food and medicine for Native Americans. The coastal Salish used the red elderberries extensively, first boiling them with hot stones, then drying them and storing them underground for winter use. Blue elderberries taste better, and Indians throughout the West ate them raw or pounded them into cakes for the winter stew pot or barbecued them over hot coals.

A medical papyrus from ancient Egyptian times confirms that *Sambucus* species have been used medicinally since 1500 B.C. Many Native American tribes used elderberry medicines. An infusion, or tincture, of bark and leaves treated a wide variety of common ailments: colds, sore throats, fevers, diarrhea, cuts, and sores. Native Americans applied poultices of chopped leaves and bark to sprains, bruises, and arthritic joints and often laid a piece of chopped bark in the hollow of an aching tooth. Blossoms brewed with peppermint leaves made a soothing tea. The *United States Pharmacopoeia* listed elderberry as an official medicine from 1831 to 1905. Modern research confirms that elderberries possess antiviral properties and may be useful in treating influenza.

Since the Roman times of Pliny, elderberry twigs have been fashioned into flutes, a craft that Native Americans also discovered. They made flutes from dried stems with hollow centers or hollowed fresh wood by pushing out the soft core of pith with a hot stick. The flutemakers then burned a single row of four or six holes for fingering the notes.

Native Americans made purple dye for coloring basketry materials from twigs, and they simmered leaves to produce light yellow or green dyes.

Pioneers, always short of fruit, made good use of blue elderberries in the kitchen, especially for juice, jam, syrup, pies, and wine. Today's foragers find them equally useful and appreciate that, unlike many wild berries, elderberries are easy to pick and prepare.

Wild Gardening: Blue elderberries grow successfully in the wild garden and are especially good for screens and windbreaks. Prune them each dormant season to keep them dense and shapely. You'll be rewarded with blooms, berries, and birds. Plants grow in USDA zones 4 and 5.

Blue Elderberry fruit   *Sambucus cerulea*

Red Elderberry fruit   *Sambucus racemosa*

Snowberries   *Symphoricarpos* species

Ten species of the often trailing snowberries, also called waxberries, grow in North America, and one species grows in China. The small leaves of these deciduous shrubs are usually elliptical or round. Flowers are bell shaped, and the berries are usually white. Thomas Jefferson was fascinated by Lewis and Clark's report of a plant that produced "berries the size of currants and literally as white as snow, which remain on the bush through the winter."

Common snowberry (S. albus) is a deciduous shrub that grows 9 feet tall. On the trunk and older branches, its smooth gray bark becomes shredded. Its oval leaves are opposite and rounded at both ends. They may be toothed or wavy lobed. White to pinkish, bell-shaped flowers bloom in racemes at or near the branch tips from May to July. The fruits are white, waxy, berrylike drupes arranged in small clusters and persisting through winter.

Common snowberry grows in much of North America up to midmountain level in moist, shady places, often in the understory of forests. Lewis and Clark discovered common snowberry as they journeyed across the Bitterroot Mountains of Montana and Idaho in the summer of 1805.

Mountain snowberry (S. oreophilus) is a small shrub growing up to 2 feet tall. It has 1-inch-long leaves and ½-inch-long, megaphone-shaped flowers that bloom in July. The ¼-inch-diameter, waxy white berries appear in September and stay attached through winter.

Mountain snowberry grows in moist places on mountain slopes from the foothills to high elevations in the Rocky Mountains and south into California, Arizona, and New Mexico.

Trailing snowberry (S. mollis) is a diffusely branched shrub less than 1 foot tall. Its round to oval leaves are lightly hairy above and covered with soft fuzzy hairs on the underside. The leaf margins are mainly smooth. Pinkish, ¼-inch-long flowers bloom in pairs or small clusters. The fruits are round and white.

Trailing snowberry grows at 3,000 to 5,000 feet in chaparral, oak woodlands, and mixed evergreen forests in the California coastal ranges, west of the Cascade Range in Oregon and Washington and east into northern Idaho.

Desert snowberry (S. longiflorus) is a low, spreading shrub with branches 1 to 2 feet long. Its elliptical leaves are sharp pointed and covered with a white bloom. Leaf margins are smooth. The flowers are pink and slightly larger than those of other *Symphoricarpos* species. Fruits are oval.

Desert snowberry prefers dry mountain slopes, mainly in pinyon-juniper woodlands in the desert mountains of northeastern California, southeastern Oregon, Colorado, and Texas.

Edibility: Snowberries are **TOXIC** if eaten in quantity, as are the leaves stems, and roots.

Historical Uses: Most Native Americans considered snowberries poisonous. Only the Squaxin of Puget Sound ate them. Several Northwest tribes believed the white berries had spirit power. Because of their white color they were thought to be ghost berries—the salmonberries of the land of the dead. A few tribes called them corpse berries. Nez Perce and southern Paiute mothers wound the branches around their cradle boards to keep ghosts away from their babies. The Makah of the Olympic Peninsula used them to counteract bad magic, and the Sechelt of coastal British Columbia used them to remove warts.

Snowberries were widely used for medicine. Many tribes used an infusion made from twigs and berries to reduce fevers and heal sores. The Paiute made poultices from boiled desert snowberry root to treat caked breasts in new mothers. The Navajo used mountain snowberry as a ceremonial emetic. Crow horsemen fed boiled and crushed roots to their horses for a laxative.

There were other uses as well. Coastal Salish-speaking tribes used snowberry leaves to make a green dye, and the Paiute and Shoshone made arrows from the young, straight wood. They cut down bushes in the fall so new shoots would grow straight up the following spring.

Wild Gardening: Snowberries are adaptable, drought-tolerant shrubs that spread by rhizomes, covering banks and other areas that are difficult to landscape. After the leaves fall, the white berries provide winter interest and attract wildlife. They grow well in USDA zones 4 to 6.

Mountain Snowberry flower
Symphoricarpos oreophilus

Trailing Snowberry fruit
Symphoricarpos mollis

Viburnums
Highbush Cranberries   *Viburnum* species

About two hundred species of *Viburnum* grow in temperate and subtropical regions around the world. Showy clusters of white, saucer-shaped flowers and colorful fruits lend ornamental value to these shrubs. Highbush cranberries resemble but are not related to the familiar Thanksgiving cranberry, which is in the heath family.

Oval-leafed viburnum (*V. ellipticum*) is a slender shrub growing from 3 to 10 feet tall. It has coarsely toothed, elliptical leaves up to 3 inches long. They are mainly smooth above, pale and slightly hairy beneath. In May and June, tiny white flowers bloom in flat clusters about 2 inches across. In late summer, oval black drupes form. The leaves turn varied shades of red in fall.

Oval-leafed viburnum is at home on the edge of wetlands, in ponderosa pine forests, and in chaparral at elevations between 1,000 and 4,000 feet. It inhabits the northern coast ranges of California, the moist region of Washington and Oregon west of the Cascade Range, and a few locations on the eastern side of the Sierra Nevada.

Squashberry (*V. edule*) is a straggly shrub, 2 to 8 feet tall, with smooth, reddish gray bark. The opposite leaves are sharply toothed and hairy beneath. They are 2 to 4 inches wide, usually with three shallow lobes toward the leaf tip. In April and May, small, white flowers bloom in clusters between pairs of leaves. Light red, oval, berrylike drupes ripen in late summer. The leaves turn crimson in the fall.

Squashberry inhabits damp woods and streambank thickets in coastal ranges from Alaska to southern Oregon and pockets of moist habitat at low to medium elevations in northern Idaho, Montana, and Colorado.

Americanbush cranberry (*V. trilobum*), also called V. *opulus* var. *americanum*, is a big, spreading shrub that may grow 15 feet tall and 12 feet wide. It has large, maplelike leaves that have three sharply toothed lobes. The inflorescence consists of a flat-topped flower cluster—an outer ring of large, white-petaled, sterile flowers surround tiny petal-less blossoms. Together they resemble a lace cap. The central cluster of tiny flowers produces round, red berries in late summer.

Americanbush cranberry grows in moist soil of low hills and plains in Washington and British Columbia and east to the Atlantic Coast.

Edibility: Fruits are edible but acidic and tart.

Historical Uses: Native Americans of the Northwest ate Americanbush cranberries wherever they were available. They usually harvested them in late fall because the berries grow sweeter after the first frost. The Indians ate some raw and mixed others with grease to store for winter use. These were often kept in birch bark baskets in an underground cache. The preserved fruit was a valuable trading item and welcome gift. Any berries left frozen on the bush

Oval-Leafed Viburnum fruit
Viburnum ellipticum

Americanbush Cranberry flowers *Viburnum trilobum*

were good for a winter nibble. The Kwakuitl of southern British Columbia sometimes harvested fresh Americanbush cranberries to serve at feasts. They picked them in bunches with stems attached. They dipped the cluster in grease, sucked the juicy pulp, and discarded the stems, seeds, and skins.

The chief medicinal use of Americanbush cranberry was to treat ailments with an infusion made from the bark. This treatment eased sore throats, colds, dysentery, and headaches.

Wild Gardening: Americanbush cranberry and its related cultivars are fashionable landscape shrubs in every season. In May, spectacular white blooms scent the garden, and in early fall bunches of shiny, red berries gleam in the sunlight. The deciduous, maplelike leaves turn red and fall, but the berries cling to the bush throughout winter, creating a stunning contrast with a snowy landscape. If you want to eat the berries, plan to get there ahead of the birds. Americanbush cranberries should be readily available at local nurseries as one variety or another will grow in USDA zones 3 to 8.

Americanbush Cranberry fruit   *Viburnum trilobum*

LAUREL FAMILY   LAURACEAE

Members of the laurel family—two thousand species of large trees and a few
shrubs—are all aromatic. They live in the tropics and warm temperate regions.
The simple, elliptical leaves may be either alternate or opposite. They have
tiny gland dots but no stipules. Small flowers of three petals and three similar
sepals form clusters along the twigs. The fruit is a berry with one large seed,
and most fruits have a collar of the flower parts around the base.

California Bay   *Umbellularia californica*

Also called Oregon myrtle, California bay is the only species in the *Umbellularia*
genus. This large, evergreen tree grows 30 to 80 feet tall and has greenish to
reddish brown bark. The shiny, dark green leaves, which smell a bit like camphor
are elliptical or lance shaped and up to 4½ inches long with edges turned
under. Pale yellow flowers are ¼ inch wide and grow at the leaf bases. The
1-inch-long, egg-shaped, greenish to dark purple fruits have large brown seeds
Flowers appear in winter from December through February, and fruits ripen
in mid to late autumn.

California bay inhabits moist canyons and valleys in chaparral, foothill
woodlands, mixed evergreen forests, and redwood forests below 5,000 feet. I
grows in the coastal ranges from southwestern Oregon to southern California
and northern Baja, and on the western slopes of the Sierra Nevada.

Edibility: Smelling crushed California bay leaves can cause a headache o
unconsciousness, and the leaves can irritate the skin. You can substitute them
in recipes for bay leaves, which come from the classic bay tree, *Laurus nobilis*
but California bay leaves are much more potent than commercial bay leaves

The seeds of California bay are edible.

Historical Uses: The Native Americans of the Pacific Coast used the leave
and wood, and ate the seed inside the berry rather than the berry itself. Th
Mendocino parched or roasted the seeds and ate them. The Pomo dried th
fruit in the sun until the skin split so they could get at the oil-rich kerne
inside. Or sometimes, they pounded the seeds into cakes and then dried ther
in the sun.

Tribes used the leaf oil to treat toothache, headache, and earache, an
to keep bugs out of stored acorns and salmon. The Salinan of southern Californi
made a leaf poultice and put it on the heads of people they considered insane
Members of several tribes breathed the crushed or burned leaves to cur
headaches. In southern California, the Cahuilla bound bay leaves on the
heads to cure headaches and took hot baths with the leaves to cure rheuma
tism. The Mendocino used the leaves to repel fleas and burned the branche
to prevent catching colds. Pomo women thought carrying a stick of Californi
bay would keep snakes away.

The light, fine-grained wood supports a tourist industry with beautifu
platters, bowls, and trays. In the past, the wood was popular for shipbuildin
and furniture.

California Bay flowers   *Umbellularia californica*

California Bay fruit   *Umbellularia californica*

LILY FAMILY   LILIACEAE

The lily family has about 240 genera and perhaps 3,000 species with a worldwide
distribution. Most of them are perennial herbs that grow from bulbs, corms,
or rhizomes. The flowers usually have six parts called tepals: three petals and
three identical sepals. The leaves are usually basal and sometimes whorled.
Some species have berries. Such familiar garden flowers as the tulip, hyacinth,
and daffodil are lilies; so are onion and garlic.

Asparagus   *Asparagus officinalis*

Asparagus, a perennial plant, grows from underground rhizomes that store the
food supply needed to power the early spring growth of its tender shoots. If
the shoots are not harvested, the plants grow to 5 or 6 feet tall. They have
thin, upward-growing branches that bear wispy twigs. The leaves are minute
scales, but the many twigs photosynthesize and thus function as leaves. Male
and female plants produce flowers in clusters of up to four. The yellowish green
flowers are ⅛ inch long and bell shaped with six identical parts: three petals
and three sepals. The female plants produce red berries, which have toxic
black seeds.

Asparagus was brought to the United States from the coasts of Europe
where many species grow. It escaped cultivation and has naturalized throughout much of North America.

Edibility: The shoots of asparagus are edible and delicious but do not eat
the berries because the seeds are **TOXIC**.

Historical Uses: Asparagus has been eaten in this country since the first
settlers arrived with roots to plant. Native Americans ate it and used it
medicinally. Because it naturalized first in the East, several eastern tribes
developed uses for it. The Cherokee drank an infusion of asparagus for rickets
and ate the shoots for rheumatism.

Asparagus grows wild along roads and irrigation canals and in unculti-
vated fields. Foragers gathering wild asparagus alongside roads and farms should
check with the landowners to be sure it hasn't been sprayed with pesticide.

Wild Gardening: Asparagus is commonly grown as a garden vegetable
though it requires special care. One-year-old root crowns transplanted out
doors should grow for two years to develop strong root systems before you harvest
the young shoots. Asparagus is very hardy and thrives in all USDA zones.

Asparagus flowers
Asparagus officinalis

Asparagus berries
Asparagus officinalis

Queencups   *Clintonia* species

These spreading perennials have two or three basal leaves and six-parted flowers—three petals and three sepals—that grow singly or in clusters. The berries are round to oblong. Six species grow in North America and Asia. The genus name, *Clintonia*, honors DeWitt Clinton, New York State governor and botanist, 1769–1828.

**Queencup (C. *uniflora)* is a perennial with two or three handsome, 6- to 8-inch-long, elliptical leaves that taper at each end. The basal cluster of leaves grows from creeping rhizomes, which form attractive colonies. In springtime the shiny, green foliage and white flowers accent moist stretches of open woods. The bractless, usually solitary flower, is about 1 inch wide and slightly cup shaped with three sepals and three petals. *Uniflora*, the species name, is from the Latin *unus*, meaning "one," and *flora*, for "flower." The flower grows erect on a slender, 6- to 10-inch-long stem. The single berry looks like a shiny, dark blue bead.

Queencup is widely abundant in moist coniferous forests throughout the Pacific Northwest and Rocky Mountains, ranging from Idaho and Montana to Colorado, Wyoming, and Utah. It can be a dominant understory species in open to shaded sites in montane to subalpine habitats.

**Red clintonia (C. *andrewsiana)* has two to five leaves and reddish flowers that grow in clusters atop a 2-foot-tall, leafless stem. Red or orange, unripe berries turn blue at maturity. Red clintonia grows in coastal forests from central California to Oregon.

Edibility: Queencup and red clintonia berries are dry, tasteless, and unpalatable, though ruffed grouse relish them.

Historical Uses: Coastal Bella Coola called queencup fruit "wolf's berry" and regarded it as unfit for human consumption. The Bella Coola and Cowlitz prepared a decoction of queencup for washing cuts and sore eyes. The Thompson tribe mashed the blue berries into a dye.

Wild Gardening: Queencups have beautiful landscaping possibilities for woodland gardens. The blossoms burst forth in spring, and the blue beads shine in fall. Queencups prefer moist, shady spots and are good companions for bunchberry, trillium, and wintergreen. Queencups grow in USDA zones 3 to 6.

Queencup blossom   *Clintonia uniflora*

Queencup berry   *Clintonia uniflora*

Fairybells   *Disporum* species

These creeping perennials have alternate leaves and white to greenish, six-parted flowers in umbels. The fruit is a round to egg-shaped, yellow or red berry. The fifteen *Disporum* species grow in temperate North America and eastern Asia.

Fairybell (*D. hookeri*) is a small, perennial herb with branched stems reaching 1 to 2 feet tall. Broad, clasping, alternate leaves are lance shaped—rounded at the base and pointed at the tips. The ingeniously shaped leaves, called "drip tips," readily capture rainwater. They are 2 to 6 inches long with pronounced parallel veins. Stems are slightly hairy, and leaves have fine hairs along the margins and upper surfaces. Creamy white, ¾-inch-long flowers usually grow in bell-shaped pairs, though they can be solitary or in threes. Almost hidden in the foliage, the flowers grow on the tips of branches, with the stamen hanging below the petals. Orange to red, egg-shaped berries are ½ inch long.

Fairybells like moist forests and subalpine meadows and inhabit mixed evergreen and redwood forests from British Columbia south to southern California and east to Idaho and Montana.

Rough-fruited fairybell (*D. trachycarpum*) resembles D. *hookeri* except that its velvety, red berries sometimes appear warty, suggesting its common name. Rough-fruited fairybell grows from British Columbia and Alberta south to New Mexico.

Fairy lantern (*D. smithii*) has smooth stems and leaves. The white, hanging flowers are arranged in clusters of two or three at the ends of the leafy stems. Unlike fairybells, the petals of the lantern-shaped flowers do not flare outward and the stamens do not hang below the lantern.

Fairy lantern grows in moist forests and meadows from British Columbia to southern California and in Montana and Idaho.

Edibility: The juicy, modestly sweet berries of fairybells are worth nibbling on walks through the woods.

Historical Uses: Most Native Americans did not eat fairybells, though several groups used them for medicine. They prepared an infusion of stems or leaves to treat wounds and sore eyes. The Makah used both fairybell and fairy lantern as a love potion. The Klallam considered them poisonous. The Nitinaht of Vancouver Island believed the berries fit only for wolves.

Wild Gardening: Fairybells grow well in moist, woodland gardens and shady borders in USDA zones 6 to 9. The delicate, drooping flowers are not flamboyant, but the handsome leaves fill in around hosta, ferns, and spring blooming bulbs. The plants spread slowly, forming colonies.

Fairybell flowers *Disporum hookeri*
—CHARLENE SIMPSON PHOTO

Fairybell fruit *Disporum hookeri*

False Solomon's Seals
False Lilies of the Valley   *Maianthemum* species

Members of the genus *Maianthemum*, which includes species formerly listed in the genus *Smilacina*, are creeping perennial herbs with alternate leaves and a panicle of flowers. The fruit is a berry. False lilies of the valley have four petal-like structures and four stamens, and false Solomon's seals have six of each. The twenty-five *Maianthemum* species grow in the Northern Hemisphere.

False Solomon's seal (M. racemosa) is a 12- to 24-inch-tall perennial that grows from fleshy rhizomes and forms colonies. Its unbranched stems can be erect or arching. The leaves are alternate, broad, elliptical, and 5 to 8 inches long. They have pronounced parallel veins and usually clasp the stem. In May and June plumes of creamy white flowers bloom at the stem ends. Juicy, orangish red berries ripen in late summer.

False Solomon's seal prefers moist woods, streambanks, and open forests from near sea level to mid elevations. It is widely distributed throughout the coastal regions from southern California to the Alaskan panhandle, on both sides of the Cascade Range, in the Sierra Nevada, and eastward to the Rocky Mountains.

Star-flowered false Solomon's seal (M. stellata) is a smaller version of false Solomon's seal. Its stems are unbranched and usually grow 12 to 18 inches long. The alternate, lance-shaped leaves grow to 6 inches long. Its star-shaped flowers are slightly larger than those of false Solomon's seal but fewer are produced. They bloom in unbranched racemes at the stem tips. The round berries ripen to purple but are greenish yellow with three to six purple stripes when immature.

Star-flowered false Solomon's seal has a similar habitat and range as false Solomon's seal but extends farther south in the Rocky Mountains to Colorado, Arizona, and Nevada.

False Lily of the Valley (M. dilatatum), a woodland beauty, is smaller than the false Solomon's seals, reaching only about 12 inches tall. It has one or two broadly heart-shaped, shiny leaves that are conspicuously veined and grow on 2- to 3-inch-long leafstalks. In May and June an elongated, terminal cluster of tiny, white flowers blooms above the leaves. Red, speckled berries replace the flowers by late summer.

False lilies of the valley are common in the coastal ranges from British Columbia to northern California and in the northern Rocky Mountains.

Edibility: Berries of false Solomon's seal and false lily of the valley are edible but unpalatable. The bitterness of false Solomon's seal berries protects us from eating enough to cause severe diarrhea—a possible reaction. No harm comes from eating young, cooked shoots of false Solomon's seal, but be sure you are not eating false hellebore (*Veratrum viride*), an extremely **TOXIC** plant that resembles false Solomon's seal.

continued on page 98

False Lily of the Valley fruit   *Maianthemum dilatatum*

False Lily of the Valley flowers   *Maianthemum dilatatum*

Historical Uses: Several northwestern Indian groups ate the berries of false lily of the valley, though they did not regard them as high-quality food. In one Haida myth, false lily of the valley was served at a feast for the gods, along with Americanbush cranberries, wild crabapples, and salal berry cakes.

Widely scattered tribes, including Paiute, Shoshone, and Maidu, developed similar uses for the two false Solomon's seals, which were used interchangeably. They produced poultices from fresh roots to treat boils or sprains and used dried, powdered root to staunch the bleeding of wounds. They boiled roots to prepare an all-purpose antiseptic wash for skin and eyes, and women brewed a contraceptive tea from the leaves. Kawaiisu fishermen carried a mixture of mashed roots to throw into the stream to stupify fish, making them easier to catch. Northwestern tribes prepared a poultice of the leaves of false lily of the valley to treat sore eyes and drank a root tea to heal internal injuries.

Modern herbalists compound false Solomon's seal roots with honey for an effective cough syrup and prepare poultices from either fresh or dried roots.

Wild Gardening: False Solomon's seal and false lily of the valley grow well in moist, woodland gardens in USDA zones 3 to 6. They colonize readily from underground stolons, and clusters of white flowers accent the base of trees and shrubs. Some specialized catalogs list false Solomon's seal, but we have not found a single source for false lily of the valley.

False Solomon's Seal flowers *Maianthemum racemosa*

Inset: False Solomon Seal berries *Maianthemum racemosa*

Star-Flowered Solomon's Seal flowers   *Maianthemum stellata*

Star-Flowered Solomon's Seal berries   *Maianthemum stellata*

Greenbriers   *Smilax* species

These perennial, climbing or trailing plants are often prickly and usually have deciduous leaves with prominent veins. White to greenish flowers grow in clusters or umbels in the leaf axils. They produce round red, black, or purple berries. Three hundred fifty species grow in the tropics, eastern Asia, and temperate North America. *Smilax* and *Aralia* are sometimes confused with each other because some species of both genera provide the flavoring sarsaparilla.

Greenbrier (*S. herbacea*) is a tangled, herbaceous thorny vine that stays green in winter. The oblong, 4-inch-long leaves have parallel veins connected by a network of branching veins. A few botanists place greenbrier in its own family because of this unusual vein pattern. Leafstalks are as long as the leaves. Small, greenish flowers appear in round clusters. Male and female flowers are borne on separate vines, and both kinds smell bad. The ⅜-inch-diameter berries are dark blue to black.

Greenbrier inhabits meadows, woods, clearings, and thickets but prefers partly open areas. It grows in the Sierra Nevada, the Midwest, and the East.

Smilax californica has a woody stem covered with brownish prickles. The 2- to 4-inch-long, deciduous leaves are egg-shaped with a sharp point. Flowers have six tiny tepals that are fused at their bases and hang in drooping umbels. This species grows along streams in coniferous forests in the Sierra foothills and north into southern Oregon.

Edibility: Greenbrier berries are edible but dry, bland, and sometimes rubbery. You can eat the leaves and shoots in spring.

Historical Uses: Few western Indians ate *Smilax* berries, but they commonly used the vines for basketry. The Indians of northern and central California wove the dark stems of *S. californica* into their baskets to make patterns. If vines were not locally available, groups like the Mendocino traveled long distances to obtain them.

Greenbrier fruit *Smilax* species —GLADYS LUCILLE SMITH,
CALIFORNIA ACADEMY OF SCIENCE

Greenbrier flower *Smilax* species
HN KALLAS PHOTO, WILD FOOD ADVENTURES

Smilax californica

Twisted Stalks   *Streptopus* species

These perennial herbs are called twisted stalks because the flower stalks have kinks in them—in some species it is a right angle, in others just a sharp curve. The leaves are oblong to ovate with pointed tips. Bell- to saucer-shaped flowers produce greenish to dark red berries. The seven species of *Streptopus* grow in North America and Eurasia.

Twisted stalk (*S. amplexifolius*) is a perennial herb with sparsely branching stems that usually reach 1 to 3 feet tall and are either arching or erect. Its leaves are alternate, broadly lance shaped, prominently veined, and 2 to 5 inches long. They clasp the stem, appearing to wrap completely around it at the leaf base. The flowers are ½-inch-long, greenish white bells that dangle from the leaf axils on short, wiry stalks. The name "twisted stalk" refers to either the distinctive kink in the flower stalks or to the main stem, which bends at each leaf node, zigzagging upward. The flowers bloom in the spring, and by midsummer, bright red, ½-inch-long, oval berries are mature.

    Twisted stalk grows in moist woods at elevations from 1,000 to 5,500 feet from California to Alaska, throughout most of the mountain West, in subalpine zones in the eastern United States, and in Canada.

Rosy twisted stalk (*S. roseus*) has an unbranched stem. Its ovate to elliptic leaves do not clasp the stem at the leaf base as does twisted stalk. Its flowers are rose colored with white tips and have curved stalks rather than kinked ones.

    Rosy twisted stalk inhabits damp woods mainly from 3,000 to 6,000 feet elevation. It grows along the West Coast from Alaska through the Olympic Mountains and Cascade Range to northern Oregon and east to southeastern British Columbia.

Edibility: Twisted stalk berries are juicy and moderately sweet. Snacking on them refreshes hikers but eating too many may cause diarrhea. The tender young shoots are tasty in spring, but resemble toxic members of the lily family such as the poisonous false hellebore (*Veratrum viride*). Because identifying leaves can be difficult, we recommend eating only the berries.

Historical Uses: Though the Thompson of British Columbia and the Okanagan of Washington ate the fresh berries, other tribes thought them fit only for snakes and frogs. Use of the twisted stalks for medicine was more widespread than use for food. They steeped chopped roots in water, creating a tonic for stomachache or loss of appetite. The Thompson tied the plant to their hair or clothing for fragrance, and the women of the Makah group chewed the roots to ease labor pains.

Wild Gardening: Twisted stalks spread readily in woodland gardens because of creeping rootstocks. They are suitable for USDA zones 3 to 6.

Twisted Stalk flowers   *Streptopus amplexifolius*

Twisted Stalk berries   *Streptopus amplexifolius*

MISTLETOE FAMILY   LORANTHACEAE

The mistletoe family is composed of about twenty genera and five hundred species of parasitic shrubs that grow on woody plants. All species of mistletoe have opposite, succulent-looking leaves or scales. The fruit is a small, often sticky berry. Mistletoes have never been successfully cultivated.

Dwarf Mistletoes   *Arceuthobium* species

Dwarf mistletoes, which are shrubs that lack chlorophyll, parasitize conifer hosts such as firs, junipers, larches, spruces, and pines. They cause an overgrowth of the host tree twigs called witches' broom. Dwarf mistletoes have scales for leaves. Solitary male and female flowers form in the scale axils on separate plants. The fruit is a berry. Though dwarf mistletoe harms its host, sapping strength and retarding growth, parasite and tree have coexisted for countless generations. Like insects and fire, dwarf mistletoe thins the forest. Dwarf mistletoe attaches to its host in a remarkable way. When the berries are ripe, they explode with great force, sending sticky seeds to adjacent conifer branches. As the sticky seed coat absorbs water from rain, the seed slips down to the base of a conifer needle. The seed puts out a disklike structure called a holdfast that sticks it to the twig. Upon germination, the root penetrates the tree.

Taxonomists sometimes classify dwarf mistletoes based on their host plant. For instance, Douglas dwarf mistletoe (*A. douglasii*) grows only on the branches of Douglas-fir (*Pseudotsuga menziesii*). Its tiny branchlets, less than 1½ inches long, grow in a fanlike arrangement.

Western dwarf mistletoe (A. *campylopodum)* has greenish brown, segmented stems that are less than 7 inches long. The leaves are small, opposite scales. Its tiny, inconspicuous flowers are yellowish orange to greenish. Sticky egg-shaped, bluish green berries ripen in late summer of the second year. Taxonomists recognize several forms of western dwarf mistletoe according to the species it parasitizes. Its host trees grow in British Columbia, the Rocky Mountains, and southern California.

Western hemlock dwarf mistletoe (A. *tsugense)* usually parasitizes western hemlock (*Tsuga heterophylla*), but it also grows on Pacific silver fir (*Abies amabilis*), subalpine fir (*A. lasioscarpa*), Noble fir (*A. procera*), and shore pine (*Pinus contorta* var. *contorta*). The fruits mature from late September to early October, thirteen to fourteen months after pollination. Western hemlock dwarf mistletoe ranges from British Columbia and Alaska south through Washington and Oregon to near Mendocino in northern California.

Edibility: Dwarf mistletoe berries are not edible and may be **TOXIC**.

Historical Uses: Okanagan women boiled Douglas-fir witches' brooms to make a hair rinse. Some California tribes used a decoction of western dwarf mistletoe for stomachache.

Western Hemlock Dwarf Mistletoe berries and swollen stem of host
Arceuthobium tsugense —DAN NICKRENT PHOTO

Mistletoes   *Phoradendron* species

Mistletoes, small woody shrubs, are tree parasites. The flowers are tiny and sunken in the axis of the flower spike. Male and female flowers usually form on separate plants. There are two hundred *Phoradendron* species in temperate and tropical North America. Mistletoe often takes the name of its host species. For example, juniper mistletoe (*P. juniperinum*) grows on Utah juniper (*Juniperus osteosperma*).

Mesquite mistletoe (*P. californicum*) is a parasitic woody plant growing on desert shrubs, primarily mesquite (*Prosopis* species). The jointed, brittle stems are approximately 20 inches long, growing in a large clump with drooping branches. The plant attaches itself to the host tree from which it obtains water and nutrients. Mesquite mistletoe appears leafless, but a close look reveals tiny scales. New stem growth is reddish in early spring. The inconspicuous, greenish flowers have no petals. The round, waxy berries progress from pinkish to white and are spread from host to host by birds.

Mesquite mistletoe thrives wherever mesquite grows in the deserts of southern Utah, Arizona, southern California, and northern Mexico.

Oak mistletoe (*P. flavescens*) parasitizes deciduous trees, mainly oaks but also cottonwoods, walnuts, and willows. Unlike mesquite mistletoe, oak mistletoe has thick, leathery, oval leaves that grow opposite on the stem. Its yellowish green, inconspicuous flowers develop into sticky, egg-shaped, pinkish white berries. Oak mistletoe grows in northern California.

Edibility: Mistletoe berries taste bad and may be **TOXIC**. Authorities are divided in their opinions of mistletoe; some say it is nontoxic, others call it poisonous.

Historical Uses: Several Indian tribes ate berries of juniper mistletoe and mesquite mistletoe when food was scarce. They made a tea from the plants to wash sores. The Navajo boiled juniper mistletoe with one-seed juniper (*Juniperus monosperma*) and pinyon (*Pinus monophylla*) to make a lotion for insect bites and to cure warts. Perhaps mistletoe's best use is still for kissing under at Christmas time.

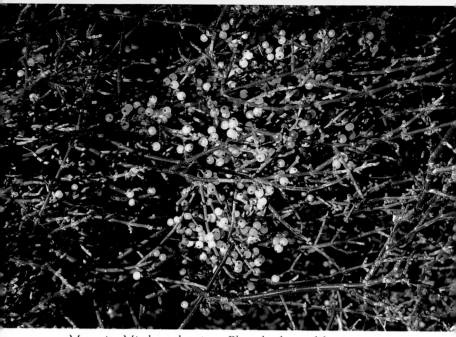

Mesquite Mistletoe berries   *Phoradendron californicum*

Mesquite Mistletoe berries   *Phoradendron californicum*

MULBERRY FAMILY   MORACEAE

The mulberry family is composed of seventy genera and one thousand species of perennial shrubs, vines, or trees with milky sap, including figs, mulberries, and breadfruit. The small, radial flowers have four petals and stamens. The fruit consists of many tiny, seedlike achenes covered by fleshy tissue.

Mulberries   *Morus* species

Mulberry was an indispensable fruit in colonial America, and generations of school children have chanted, "Here we go round the mulberry bush." Perhaps because of its universality, "Operation Mulberry" was chosen as the code name for an engineering feat that resulted in the successful landing of Allied troops on the beaches of Normandy during World War II. Silkworms, the caterpillars that produce silk, eat mulberry leaves. White mulberry *(Morus alba)*, or silkworm tree, has been the basis of China's silk industry since ancient times.

The twelve species of mulberries grow in warm and temperate regions of the Northern Hemisphere. Only two are native to the United States. All mulberries have alternate, sharply toothed, heart-shaped leaves and small, greenish flowers that hang in catkins. The male and female flowers are usually on separate trees. Milky sap in the leaves and stems may irritate the skin. The fruit resembles a blackberry but the seeds are enclosed in a hard coat.

Western mulberry (M. *microphylla*) is a native shrub or small tree, with thin, gray bark tinged with red. It usually grows to a height of 12 to 15 feet, with an open, irregular shape. The heart-shaped, alternate leaves are 1 to 2 inches long with sharp-toothed edges. The upper surfaces are dull dark green and somewhat rough; underneath they are smooth to somewhat hairy. In April, tiny, green flowers appear in hanging spikes ½ to ¾ inch long. The female spikes develop into ½-inch-long, oblong berries that are an aggregate of many beadlike, one-seeded, purple drupes. They usually ripen in June.

Western mulberry grows on dry hillsides and canyons of southern New Mexico, southern Arizona, adjacent Mexico, and western Texas.

White mulberry (M. *alba*), a large tree introduced from Asia, grows to 80 feet. Its glossy, green leaves are ovate and 4 inches long. They are coarsely toothed and often lobed. White mulberry has become somewhat naturalized in the Southwest. A few states prohibit its cultivation because some people are allergic to its pollen.

Edibility: Mulberry fruits are edible and delicious. They vary from sweet and juicy to quite tart and are excellent in jelly.

Historical Uses: Southwestern Indians ate fresh or dried mulberries. Several groups used them as a laxative, and some prepared a drink to reduce fevers. Few other medicinal uses are known.

Southwestern tribes sometimes used the stems for basketry and to make hunting bows. To make a bow, the Papago cut a straight limb—5 feet long and 2 inches thick—during the rainy season, peeled off the bark, and rubbed the rough spots down with a stone. They tapered each end to 1 inch in diameter and notched it. After placing it in hot ashes to bend the ends up gradually, they strung the bow with a fine strip of deerhide.

Wild Gardening: Mulberry trees offer shade, beauty, and berries, which birds love. The long fruiting season usually provides plenty of berries for birds and gardeners alike. Mulberries grow in USDA zones 4 to 6.

White Mulberry fruit   *Morus alba*
—VIRGINIA WEINLAND PHOTO, PHOTO RESEARCHERS, INC.

NIGHTSHADE FAMILY   SOLANACEAE

The nightshade, or potato, family has about two thousand species, most of which grow in tropical climates. Several species are native to the West. Economically important species include eggplants, green and red peppers, tomatoes, potatoes, and tobacco.

Boxthorns   *Lycium* species

Lycium species have spiny branches, succulent leaves, and tubular, greenish to purple flowers. Botanists often disagree on their classification. More than one hundred species grow in warm, dry regions all around the world.

Anderson's wolfberry (*L. andersonii*) is a much-branched, rounded shrub with slightly fuzzy stems and needlelike spines. It grows about 4 or 5 feet tall and 3 feet wide. The succulent leaves are shaped like spatulas and are less than 1 inch long. They grow in clusters of two to five. The white to purplish flowers form narrow tubes, often no longer than ½ inch. It has small, oval, red berries. Anderson's wolfberry occupies dry, stony mesas below 6,000 feet in creosote bush scrub, pinyon-pine woodlands, sagebrush scrub, chaparral, and coastal sage scrub. It grows in the Mojave and Sonoran Deserts, occasionally west of the Sierra Nevada in southern California, and in Utah and New Mexico.

Rabbitbush (*L. brevipes*) is a spreading, irregularly branched shrub that may reach 3 to 10 feet tall. Oval to spatulate leaves are up to 1 inch long and grow in clusters. The cream to lavender flowers are funnel shaped, and the fruit is a round, bright red berry.

Rabbitbush prefers washes and hillsides at elevations below 1,500 feet. It grows in southeastern California and northern Mexico.

Pale wolfberry (*L. pallidum*) is a spiny, 2- to 6-foot-tall shrub whose leaves have a thin, waxy covering that make them look grayish green. The flowers are ½ to ¾ inch long, trumpet shaped, and ³⁄₁₆ inch or more in diameter at the flared end. They are white to lavender and produce a round, reddish blue berry with a whitish, waxy coat.

Pale wolfberry grows on dry, rocky hills below 2,500 feet in the central and western Mojave Desert.

Edibility: You can eat boxthorn berries raw, cooked, or dried. Some berries are sweet; others are dry and bitter.

 Lycium Sauce, page 201

Historical Uses: Many Native Americans ate boxthorn berries and considered stewed and sweetened berries a delicacy. If the berries were bitter, they sometimes mixed them with clay to cut the tartness. The little, red berries were a staple food for the Paiute of Owens Valley, California, who ate them fresh or dried and ground into meal. Berries were also mashed and boiled with water to make juice or sweetened for pancake syrup. Pima women still process boxthorns as well as several other *Lycium* species. A harvest of 20 to 30 pounds per family is not unusual. The abundant berries of rabbitbush were important in the diets of many Southwestern Indian tribes, particularly the Hopi, Zuni, and Cahuilla. Today, they are used much like tomatoes.

Traditionally, the Navajo and Zuni communities used *Lycium* plants medicinally—ground roots for toothaches and an infusion of bark and leaves for healing cuts and for a general tonic. Zuni farmers still plant bits of soaked, pale wolfberry roots with corn seed to discourage worms and promote faster growth.

Rabbitbush blossoms   *Lycium brevipes*

Rabbitbush berry
Lycium brevipes

Groundcherries   *Physalis* **species**

Annual and perennial groundcherries spread by rhizomes. The leaves are opposite or alternate. Spots often cover the inside of the usually bell-shaped, yellowish flowers. The round fruit is a berry with many tiny seeds. All groundcherries have an inflated, papery calyx that encloses the yellow fruit and looks like a miniature Chinese lantern. Eighty-five species grow in North America, Eurasia, and Australia, some cultivated for edible fruit. Distinguishing groundcherry species from each other is difficult.

Groundcherry (*P. virginiana*) is a perennial herb about 2 feet tall, with branched stems. The leaves are 2 to 3 inches long and lance shaped, with either smooth or bluntly toothed margins. Lower leaves are alternate, but the upper ones, where the flowers are borne, may be paired. Flowers are yellow with dark centers and form a hanging bell, the rim of which is barely divided into lobes. The fruit matures to a round, yellow berry, about ¾ inch in diameter, with many tiny, tomato-like seeds. It is completely enclosed in the papery calyx. When the fruit approaches ripeness, the green lantern drops to the ground and the berry continues to ripen in the husk. The plants fruit and flower at the same time, from April to November.

Groundcherry prefers moist to medium dry, open areas—roadsides, ditches, waste areas, and cultivated ground. Widely distributed in North America, it grows throughout the intermountain West.

Wright's groundcherry (*P. wrightii*) resembles groundcherry but grows to 5 feet and has white flowers and 2- to 5-inch-long, irregularly toothed leaves. **Lance-leafed groundcherry (*P. lanceifolia*)** resembles Wright's groundcherry except that its leaves can be smooth or only slightly toothed. *P. ixocarpa*, the tomatillo popular in Mexican cooking, yields 1-inch-diameter fruits that completely fill the husk. These three species like dry areas and grow in the Southwest from Texas to California and in Mexico.

Edibility: Sweet and juicy, groundcherries are worth foraging when hiking. You can eat them fresh off the bush or pick them up off the ground where they fall and finish ripening. The berries are ripe when they turn golden. Raw, green ones are **TOXIC**, but cooking destroys the toxin.

Groundcherry Crockpot Stew, page 191
Groundcherry Chutney, page 200

Historical Uses: Pioneers used groundcherries for preserves and pies, and many southwestern Native Americans considered them a staple food. The Zuni cooked the berries into a condiment, and the Navajo dried and ground them into flour. Tomatillos are indispensable for Mexican cuisine and are often grown as a garden tomato. The papery lanterns are popular with modern crafters as the husks dry naturally.

Groundcherry flowers   *Physalis virginiana*

Groundcherry fruit   *Physalis virginiana*

Bittersweets
Nightshades   *Solanum* species

The *Solanum* genus contains fifteen hundred species of annuals, shrubs, and vines. Many are cultivated for food, including the potato, and many are partly or entirely toxic. A couple of native species grow in the mountains of Utah and Colorado, but others in the West have been introduced from eastern and central North America, South America, and Eurasia. The leaves are often lobed, and the flowers are white to purple, flared bells. The fruit of some species is a many-seeded berry.

Bittersweet (*S. dulcamara*), also called nightshade, is an introduced, semiwoody vine that readily climbs trees or sprawls on the ground. It spreads by rhizomes and seeds and can become a nuisance. The ovate leaves are shaped like arrowheads and 2 to 4 inches long. The purplish flowers have five petals, sometimes bent backward, that are fused at the base to form a short tube from which protrudes a yellow cone of anthers. The flower resembles a shooting star or tomato blossom. Its fruits are bright red, round to oval berries. Flowers and fruits appear together from approximately April to October. The species scientific name is from the Latin *dulca,* meaning "sweet" and *mara,* meaning "bitter."

Bittersweet was introduced from Europe and has naturalized across most of North America in disturbed, cultivated, or waste sites. It grows in moist shaded places in the Northwest, often invading riparian shrublands.

Black nightshade (*S. nigrum*), also called deadly nightshade, is a bushy annual about 2 feet high. The oval leaves are smooth to wavy edged, tapered to the tip, and sometimes edged with purple. It has white to pale blue flowers whose petals bend abruptly backward or downward. They resemble those of the potato and tomato. Red berries turn black when mature.

Black nightshade, introduced from Europe, grows in moist, shaded locations below 7,000 feet throughout the West and is a troublesome weed around cultivated fields.

Edibility: Do not eat the **TOXIC** berries of bittersweet, black nightshade, or other *Solanum* species.

Historical Uses: Native Americans, particularly those in the Southwest, have occasionally eaten *Solanum* berries, and some pioneers used them in pies. Cooking reportedly destroys the toxins. Great Basin tribes sometimes made a tea from dried nightshade berries when traveling in areas where water was not potable. The Maidu made a poultice of leaves to relieve body aches and pains. Black nightshade juice was used to color tattoos.

rsweet flowers *Solanum dulcamara*

Bittersweet berries *Solanum dulcamara*

Bittersweet berries *Solanum dulcamara*

OLEASTER FAMILY   ELAEAGNACEAE

Oleasters are spiny shrubs or trees whose twigs, fruits, and undersides of leaves are covered with tiny scales or hairs. The deciduous leaves are alternate, opposite, or whorled with no teeth or stipules. Flowers are small and form singly or in clusters at the leaf bases. They can be bisexual or have male and female flowers on the same or separate plants. They have a tubular or saucer-shaped, four-lobed calyx but no petals. Four to eight stamens and one pistil are attached above the flower.

Buffaloberries   *Shepherdia* species

There are only three *Shepherdia* species, all native to western North America. The shrubs have opposite leaves, and male and female flowers form on different plants. The tiny female flowers are urn shaped with a caplike stigma, and the male flowers are saucer shaped with eight stamens.

Soopolallie (*S. canadensis*), also called soapberry, is an 8-foot-tall shrub or small tree with no thorns. Its twigs and the undersides of leaves are covered with brown scales. The opposite leaves are elliptical, less than 2 inches long, and an intense dark green. Tiny, chartreuse flowers grow in clusters in the leaf axils. Male and female flowers are borne on separate plants. They bloom in April and May at low elevations and in June in the mountains. Female trees bear 1/4-inch-diameter, red to yellow, oval berries that are translucent. They ripen in July at low elevations and in early August in the mountains. The roots of soopolallie have nodules of nitrogen-fixing bacteria similar to plants in the legume family.

female

Soopolallie prefers well-drained soils in open areas or woods and often grows along streams or in washes. It ranges from Alaska to Oregon and east to the Atlantic Coast.

male fl

Buffaloberry (*S. argentea*) is a deciduous shrub or tree up to 20 feet tall with shaggy bark and thorns on the ends of its branches. Star-shaped scales on the twigs and both sides of the leaves give it a silvery look. Yellowish flowers appear before the leaves. Male flowers have four sepals and eight stamens, and the sepals of the female flowers form a cup around the pistil. Female flowers bear oval, red to yellow, 1/4-inch-diameter berries.

Two other shrubs resemble buffaloberry. If a shrub is silvery with alternate leaves and no thorns it may be silverberry (*Eleagnus commutata*). A similar *Eleagnus* is the thorny, introduced Russian olive. Its leaves are narrower than those of buffaloberry and silverberry, and its fruit is grayish.

continued on page 11

olallie flower and leaf buds
Shepherdia canadensis

Soopolallie flowers
Shepherdia canadensis

Soopolallie berries   *Shepherdia canadensis*

Lewis and Clark discovered buffaloberry at the mouth of the Niobrara River in South Dakota. Buffaloberry grows along river banks and in valleys across western Canada and south to California, New Mexico, Kansas, and Minnesota. It does not grow in Washington, Idaho, or western Montana.

Roundleaf buffaloberry (*S. rotundifolia*) has round, silvery leaves, and its fruit is covered with silvery scales. It grows in Utah, Colorado, and Arizona.

Edibility: Soopolallie berries are edible but bitter. Flavor improves after the first frost and when cooked, but if eaten in quantity they can cause intestinal distress. Buffaloberries are much better tasting than soopolallie berries, but the thorny bushes discourage foraging.

Buffaloberry-Apple Crisp, page 187
Indian Ice Cream, page 189

Buffaloberry berries   *Shepherdia argentea*
—JAMES R. JOHNSON PHOTO, SOUTH DAKOTA STATE UNIVERSITY

Historical Uses: Native Americans whipped raw soopolallie berries with water to make a meringuelike dessert that settlers called Indian ice cream. The berries foam when whipped because they contain the chemical saponin, often used commercially as a foaming agent. Tribes stirred serviceberries, salal berries, or camas bulbs into the whipped dessert to sweeten it. After the settlers arrived with modern staples, Indians added cream and sugar. Since the berries could be very bitter even when sweetened, the dessert was usually eaten as a topping as we use whipped cream. Settlers and Native Americans also utilized the foaming property of soopolallie to make soap.

Buffaloberries were a staple food for many Native Americans. They ate the fresh berries, boiled them in puddings, made jelly, and dried them for winter. Sometimes the Indians harvested the berries by placing animal hides beneath the shrubs and then beating the branches so the berries fell onto the hides. Other times the berries were eaten right off the bush. John Muir noticed a group of berry pickers at Mono Lake, California. He wrote in his journal of the Indian men who were, "feasting on buffalo berries, lying beneath the tall bushes now red with fruit. The berries are rather insipid, but they must needs be wholesome, since for days and weeks the Indians, it is said, eat nothing else." Pioneer women made jelly of these berries to serve with meat and planted the bushes as windbreaks.

Native Americans devised many medicinal uses for soopolallie. Several groups boiled leaves and bark to make a tea for treating multiple ailments—fevers, diarrhea, tuberculosis, and sore eyes—and for easing labor pains. A similar decoction was used to wash gonorrhea sores. The Thompson drank the berry juice for boils and prescribed the frothy "ice cream" for heart attacks. They also purified themselves in their sweathouses with a decoction of the stems and leaves. The Carrier made a brown hair dye from boiled branches. It had the side effect of curling their hair.

Buffaloberry had medicinal uses as well. The Crow mixed cooked berry juice with blackstrap molasses for cough medicine. The Blackfeet ate the berries as a laxative.

Wild Gardening: Any *Shepherdia* is a good, low- to medium-size shrub for drier gardens. Buffaloberry is particularly drought resistant and also tolerant of extreme cold, growing in USDA zones 2 and 3. Buffaloberry has attractive, silvery foliage, but it also has thorns. For any species, buy a shrub of each sex to get berries.

PALM FAMILY   ARECACEAE

The palm family of two hundred genera and three thousand species is present throughout the tropics, and some species are native to warm parts of North America. Only one species is native to the United States, where it is restricted to isolated colonies in California and Arizona. The trunks are generally erect and unbranched. Leaves are palmately or pinnately compound.

California Fan Palm   *Washingtonia filifera*

California fan palm grows from 20 to 40 feet tall or taller, with an unbranched trunk 1 to 2 feet in diameter, which can be even larger in cultivation. The columnar trunk is covered with a dense mass of pendant, dead leaf fans that lose their shape as they dry. The fan-shaped leaves cluster near the top of the trunk and grow up to 6 feet long and nearly as broad. They are composed of many accordion folds that are slashed about halfway or more from the tip of the leaf to the base. Threadlike fibers hang from the margins of each leaf segment. The leafstalk can be 3 or more feet long, with spiny margins. In May and June, small, white, bisexual flowers bloom in compound clusters 8 to 10 feet long that grow from the axils of the upper leaves. In August and September, black, berrylike drupes form in large clusters along the stalk. Each ¼-inch-diameter drupe has a thin, sweet pulp.

Groves of California fan palms occupy moist alkaline spots around seeps and springs below 3,500 feet elevation in southern California, southern Arizona, and Baja. Native groves grow at Palm Canyon near Palm Springs, California; at Thousand Palms Canyon near Indio, California; in the canyons of the Kofa

California Fan Palm flowers
Washingtonia filifera
—PHOTO TAKEN AT RANCHO
SANTA ANA BOTANIC GARDEN

California Fan Palm fruit
Washingtonia filifera
—PHOTO TAKEN AT RANCHO
SANTA ANA BOTANIC GARDEN

Mountains in Arizona; and in portions of the Salton Sea basin. An impressive grove thrives at Rancho Santa Ana Botanic Garden in Claremont, California.

Edibility: Fan palm fruit is edible and sweet.

Historical Uses: Southwestern Native Americans, particularly the Cahuilla, harvested large quantities of fan palm fruit. To harvest the big, grapelike clusters that might be 40 feet above the ground, the Cahuilla devised a long pole with a crossbar on the end. With it they cut off the clusters, which then fell to the ground. They collected several hundred pounds of fruit per year this way. Native Americans ate the sweet berries raw, or dried them in the sun and stored them for future use. The dried fruits, including the seeds, were ground into a meal for bread or porridge or were soaked in water to make a beverage. The desert peoples used the fibrous leaves for waterproof and windproof thatch on homes and shelters, replacing it annually. They used the fiber to weave baskets, cordage, nets, and skirts. Stem wood was used for flailing and hulling dried seedpods and in constructing tools and cooking items. Seeds were used for ceremonial gourd rattles.

Fan palms grow only near water, so groves were ideal camping spots. Sometimes palm groves were "owned" communally by several Cahuilla families, or a single family might claim an individual tree. Fruits and fronds were used in trade with distant tribes.

Wild Gardening: Fan palms have long been cultivated and are excellent shade trees in the hot, sunny climate of USDA zone 8.

California Fan Palm trees   *Washingtonia filifera*
—PHOTO TAKEN AT RANCHO SANTA ANA BOTANIC GARDEN

Inset: California Fan Palm leaf   *Washingtonia filifera*
—PHOTO TAKEN AT RANCHO SANTA ANA BOTANIC GARDEN

ROSE FAMILY ROSACEAE

The large rose family consists of about one hundred widely distributed genera
and two thousand species of herbs, shrubs, and trees. The family is composed
of such important fruiting and ornamental shrubs of temperate climates as
chokecherry, crabapple, hawthorn, Indian plum, mountain ash, raspberry, blackberry, serviceberry, strawberry, toyon, and wild rose. The leaves are alternate,
usually simple, and have paired stipules. Stems may or may not be prickly. The
bisexual flowers usually have five sepals, five petals, and many stamens.

Serviceberries *Amelanchier* species

Ten *Amelanchier* species, all shrubs or trees, grow in temperate North America,
Eurasia, and North Africa. The bark is gray to reddish brown, and the leaves
are alternate or clustered. Urn- or bell-shaped flowers appear in racemes or
clusters. The fruit is a bluish black, berrylike pome.

Serviceberry (A. alnifolia), also called saskatoon, is a spreading shrub or
small tree, varying from 3 to 20 feet tall. Branches are smooth, though shallow
furrows roughen the reddish to gray bark when mature. Young stems are reddish.
The deciduous leaves are alternate, generally oval, and 1 to 2 inches long with
rounded tips. They are sharply toothed only above the middle. They turn shades
of yellow, orange, and reddish brown in fall. From April to June, serviceberries
brighten the hillsides with a lavish bloom. The white flowers grow in clusters
at the branch tips. Each blossom has five sepals and five slender petals that
twist just enough to look disheveled. If you see a symmetrical, prim, four-petaled
flower, you may be looking at syringa (*Philadelphus lewisii*), which is often
confused with serviceberry. Stamens number fifteen to twenty. Small ¼- to
½-inch-diameter fruits appear in early summer, dull red at first, then turning
purple but slightly misted with a bluish bloom. Though the fruits are called
berries, they are constructed like miniature apples.

On the Pacific Coast, serviceberry is highly variable
and botanists do not agree if it is one species or several.
Coastal populations are sometimes referred to as
A. *florida.* When Meriwether Lewis recorded
"servicebury" in his expedition journal it was a
plant new to science.

Serviceberry is widely dispersed throughout
the West where it grows along moist streambanks,
in meadows, on dry hillsides, and on talus slopes
from sea level to subalpine regions. It is common
in the coastal ranges from southern Alaska to
California, in Washington and Oregon, in the
Sierra Nevada, and in the Rocky Mountains of
Montana, Idaho, Utah, Colorado, New Mexico,
and Arizona.

continued on page 12

Serviceberry fruit   *Amelanchier alnifolia*

Serviceberry flowers   *Amelanchier alnifolia*

Great Basin serviceberry (A. utahensis), another well-known species in the West, differs from serviceberry in that it is bushier, reaches only 3 to 9 feet tall, and its leaves are smaller and pubescent on both sides.

It is common in the Great Basin, growing on dry plains and hills from Idaho to Colorado and south to New Mexico and California. It prefers elevations of 5,000 to 7,000 feet.

Pale serviceberry (A. pallida) grows only 3 to 6 feet tall, with short, rigid, grayish branches. Its leaves are pale green and its fruit is reddish, eventually darkening to purple.

Pale serviceberry grows on dry hillsides below 11,000 feet, particularly in the coniferous forests of the coast ranges and the Sierra Nevada, and in Oregon and western Nevada.

Edibility: Serviceberries can be sweet, juicy, or seedy and are good either raw or cooked. Size, texture, and taste vary considerably depending on the season, the individual plant, and the locality. If there's been plenty of moisture, the berries can be plump and juicy.

Serviceberry-Lemon Tea Bread, page 182
Mom's Serviceberry Squares, page 185
Serviceberry Jam, page 196
Mixed Fruit Compote, page 198
Mixed Berry Syrup, page 203
Spiced Pemmican, page 206

Historical Uses: Generations of Native Americans, fur traders, and pioneers relied on serviceberries to add variety to an often monotonous diet. Pioneer women made pies and jam. Indians ate serviceberries raw and dried them like raisins for trail food and winter use. Many groups pounded and mixed the berries with dried meat to make pemmican. The Nez Perce made pudding, and many western tribes used them to flavor stew. Serviceberries were so important to the Shuswap of British Columbia that they called the eighth month, or moon "saskatoons ripen." Many tribes used the dried berries as goods for trade.

The Nez Perce, Flathead, Chinook, and probably others, crushed the fruit added a few seeds and roots, and shaped the mixture into large loaves. Some loaves were estimated to weigh as much as 15 pounds. When dried, piece could be broken off and eaten dry or tossed into the soup. The Ute made an imaginative fruitcake using dried serviceberries and pulverized grasshoppers. For inland northwestern tribes such as the Blackfeet and Nespelem, extra berrie were used in trade with the coastal Indians.

Serviceberries had limited medicinal use though the Shoshone made a solution from green inner bark, simmered in water, to treat snow blindness. The Blackfeet used a decoction of twigs and leaves for colds and stomach upsets The Nespelem, Thompson, and Pomo treated problems of pregnancy and childbirth with a similar mixture.

Almost universally throughout the West, Native Americans used the hard serviceberry wood to make arrows, spears, digging sticks, baby carriers, and sturdy basket rims. The Achomawi and Modoc of California wore a protective armor of the wood when fighting. The Maidu thatched their houses with serviceberry branches and produced a purple dye from the ripe berries.

Wild Gardening: Serviceberry is a natural choice for the wild gardener. This handsome ornamental shrub boasts a profuse bloom, colorful fruit, orangish yellow autumn foliage, and attractive bark. And birds love it! Serviceberry is relatively pest free in cool climates, but in warmer areas, it is susceptible to problems common to members of the rose family. It is hardy in USDA zones 3 to 5. Serviceberry, as well as several new horticultural varieties, are readily available from plant nurseries.

Hawthorns   *Crataegus* species

The genus name *Crataegus* comes from the Greek *kratos*, meaning "strength," which refers to the strong wood. The "haw" in hawthorn is old English for hedge. More than one hundred hawthorn species live in the United States but they are difficult to distinguish because they hybridize. Only four species are native to the West, though eastern and midwestern species have been planted in and near civilized areas.

Black hawthorn (*C. douglasii*), also called thorn apple, is a thorny shrub or tree that can reach 30 feet tall. Its straight thorns are up to 1 inch long and make hawthorn thickets impenetrable. The glossy leaves, which alternate on the stem, are oval, 1 to 3 inches long, and broadest toward the tip. The margins are sawtoothed, with five to nine shallow lobes around the tip. In autumn, the leaves turn red. White flowers bloom in rounded clusters in April and May. They have ten pretty pink stamens but smell like a dead animal. The ¼- to ½-inch-diameter berry looks like a tiny apple but is purple to black with large seeds.

Black hawthorn prefers moist soil in woods, thickets, along streams, and at the edges of meadows. It grows in Alaska, across Canada, and in the northern United States as far east as the Great Lakes and as far south as California.

Columbia hawthorn (*C. columbiana*) has thorns up to 2½ inches long, and the berries are dark red and egg-shaped. Columbia hawthorn grows east of the Cascade Range to Idaho, Montana, and Wyoming.

River hawthorn (*C. rivularis*), sometimes listed as a variety of black hawthorn (var. *erythropoda*), has smooth to slightly fuzzy leaves that are narrower than those of black hawthorn. The fruit is red to purple or black. River hawthorn grows from Wyoming to southern Idaho and south to New Mexico and Arizona.

Suksdorf hawthorn (*C. suksdorfii*) resembles black hawthorn, except it has shorter thorns, its leaves are less often lobed, and it has twenty stamens. Some botanists list it as a variety of black hawthorn (var. *suksdorfii*). Suksdorf hawthorn grows at higher elevations than black hawthorn, but it is so similar to black hawthorn that thorn length is the best way to distinguish the two species.

Edibility: Hawthorn berries are edible but taste sweet, insipid, bitter, or astringent, varying from tree to tree.

Historical Uses: Hawthorn berries were not a choice food for many Native Americans. Some tribes didn't eat the berries at all except in times of famine. To make the berries taste better they often mixed them with grease or salmon oil. Inland tribes dried the fruits and then ground them into flour for winter. Sometimes the berries were added to pemmican, particularly if the service berry crop failed. The Nez Perce often made hawthorn berry cakes. The Okanagan also made berry cakes and dipped them into deer marrow soup like

Black Hawthorn flower   *Crataegus douglasii*

Black Hawthorn fruit   *Crataegus douglasii*

tortilla chips. The Coeur d'Alene boiled the berries in baskets and then spread them on grass to dry, pouring the juice over them from time to time until it also dried. The Comanche chewed the inner bark like gum.

Before eating hawthorn, the Blackfeet thought it was necessary to give the tree gifts to prevent stomach cramps. Boys gave the trees miniature bows and arrows made from the thorns, and girls gave the trees tiny moccasins.

Coastal tribes used hawthorns medicinally, treating heart disease, venereal disease, dysentery, and stomach trouble with infusions of bark. Thorns were used for making rakes to catch herring and for lancing boils and piercing ears. The natives carved excellent tool handles and weapons from the strong hawthorn wood. In Montana, tribes made sticks for digging camas (*Camassia quamash*).

Pioneers used hawthorn berries for jam and jelly and in home medicine. They administered an infusion of black hawthorn bark for diarrhea, for a uterine tonic, and for strengthening the heart.

Wild Gardening: The dense foliage, spring flowers, and bright fruits of hawthorns add interest to almost any landscape. They are easy to grow and adaptable to tough conditions, including city pollution. A wide selection of species and cultivars is generally available and thrives in USDA zones 4 to 6.

Columbia Hawthorn fruit   *Crataegus columbiana*

Columbia Hawthorn flower   *Crataegus columbiana*

Wild Strawberries   *Fragaria* species

Wild strawberries are creeping perennial plants with toothed basal leaves and five-petaled, white flowers with at least twenty stamens. The fleshy, red fruit is not a berry but an aggregate of pistils and achenes, which are seeds with woody coats. The seeds partially cover the fruit. There are about thirty *Fragaria* species, all growing in northern temperate regions.

Strawberries spread by long stems called stolons or runners. Some people say the plants were called strawberries because people used to lay straw around them to keep mud off the berries. Others say the name came from the plant's habit of spreading or strewing runners over the ground.

Woodland strawberry (*F. vesca*) has compound basal leaves, each with three yellowish green leaflets that are thin, hairy, scalloped, toothed, and strongly veined. The surface of the leaflet bulges up between the veins, and the end tooth on the leaflet is larger than the other teeth. The white flowers have five petals, each about ½ inch across, with twenty or more stamens and many pistils fused together at the end of the stem. In two varieties (*F. vesca* var. *bracteata* and var. *crinita*) the tiny seeds are partly sunken in the berry rather than on the surface.

Woodland strawberry grows in meadows, on streambanks, and in light woods across the United States.

Mountain strawberry (*F. virginiana*) differs from woodland strawberry in that the terminal tooth of the leaflets is smaller than those next to it, and the leaf surface is not bulged between the veins. Its leaves, which are bigger than its flowers, are bluish green on top. Seeds coat the surface of the berry, which may be flattened on one side. It usually ripens in August.

Mountain strawberry grows in open woods and meadows in the lower elevations of mountains across the United States, mainly east of the Cascade Range.

Beach strawberry (*F. chiloensis*) has hairy runners connecting the plants, thick leathery leaflets that turn reddish in winter, and 1½-inch-wide flowers. You can distinguish it by its wrinkled, upper leaf surface and netted veins and hairs on the undersides of the leaves. The seeds are in pits on the surface of the berry. Berries appear from April through June.

Beach strawberry grows on bluffs and sand dunes along the Pacific Coast from Alaska to South America.

Edibility: Wild strawberries are delicious, but it is hard to find enough at one time to cook with them. The woodland strawberry has less flavor than the mountain or beach strawberries.

Nancy's Strawberry-Blueberry Muffins, *page 180*
Wild Strawberry Waffle Breakfast, *page 182*
Raspberry-Strawberry Freezer Jam, *page 196*
Mixed Fruit Compote, *page 198*
Wild Strawberry Shrimp Salad, *page 199*

continued on page 132

Woodland Strawberry flower   *Fragaria vesca*

Woodland Strawberry fruit   *Fragaria vesca*

Historical Uses: Native Americans regarded wild strawberries as a choice food. The Dakota even named the lunar month of June, "the moon when strawberries are ripe." Some tribes in central California used strawberries in annual ceremonies to honor spring. The Gitksan of British Columbia boiled the berries and spread them out in cakes on thimbleberry leaves to dry in the sun or on racks over a fire.

Native Americans used the leaves and fruit medicinally. They chewed the leaves into a poultice for burns. The Skokomish, Blackfeet, and Digueño used a tea made from the entire plant to cure diarrhea. The Thompson made pads from the leaves to wear in their armpits for deodorant. Strawberry was a Navajo "life medicine," a plant they gave decoctions of to injured people as an emergency medicine.

From early times, herbalists prescribed strawberry as a tonic for the female reproductive system. They used tea from the leaves for eczema, for inflammations of the mouth and eyes, and for diarrhea and stomach upsets. Today, herbal teas often contain strawberry leaves, which are rich in vitamin C. Leaves and berries are added to cosmetics to close pores and tighten the skin.

Wild Gardening: Wild strawberries make charming groundcovers beneath delphiniums and roses because they spread rapidly with runners. Some wild strawberries should be available from local nurseries. Most cultivated berries are variants of *F. chiloensis*. Wild species grow in USDA zones 3 to 7.

Mountain Strawberry flowers   *Fragaria virginiana*

Toyon   *Heteromeles arbutifolia*

Toyon, the only species in the *Heteromeles* genus, is a small, evergreen tree with 2- to 4-inch-long, narrow leaves that are shiny, dark green on top and pale green underneath. They are thick, oblong, and toothed. Only one main vein shows clearly. The gray bark is aromatic, and young branches are woolly. In June and July, ¼-inch-wide, white flowers bloom in large, flattish sprays at the ends of the branches. The flowers have ten stamens and five petals. The ¼- to ⅜-inch-diameter, bright red berries resemble little apples, though some trees bear yellow berries. The beautiful berries stay attached through February and are used as Christmas decorations in California. Toyon is also called Christmas berry, California holly, and hollywood. The hills above Hollywood were once thick with the town's namesake tree.

Toyon inhabits dry, rich soil and brushy slopes. It grows up to 3,500 feet elevation in the Sierra foothills, in the coast ranges of California, and on hills in Nevada.

Edibility: Raw toyon berries are sour, bitter, and astringent, but cooking is said to remove some of the bitter taste. Some authors say toyon leaves, berries, and seeds contain cyanide compounds that make them poisonous. However, Native Americans, Spanish settlers, and pioneers all used the berries.

Historical Uses: California natives ate the berries roasted, boiled, or raw. They often boiled them and then baked the boiled berries in a pit for a couple of days. Or they stored the berries for several weeks until they were soft and then parched them with coals. The Maidu, as well as early Spanish settlers in California, made cider from them. The Spanish also boiled the fruit or sprinkled it with sugar and baked it.

Several native groups made an infusion of toyon bark and leaves to drink for a blood purifier, to relieve aches and pains, and to treat infected wounds. The Costanoan of California used the infusion to induce abortion.

Toyon wood was used for arrows, tools, and ornaments. Chumash men wore a 15-inch-long, wood hairpin that held their hair in a bun.

Wild Gardening: Toyon is an elegant landscape tree in warm climates and helps control erosion. As a hedge, it does not require pruning, but it produces more berries if cut back every year. Nurseries usually recommend USDA zone 8 for best growth.

Toyon flowers   *Heteromeles arbutifolia*

Left: Toyon berries
Heteromeles arbutifolia

ight: Toyon tree with berries
Heteromeles arbutifolia

Western Crabapple   *Malus fusca*

Some botanists put western crabapple in the pear genus, classifying it *Pyrus fusca*. This tree grows up to 30 feet tall, often with several trunks and a contorted crown. The bark on the trunk is rough, gray, and fissured. Its short branches are sometimes tipped with thorny spikes. The alternate leaves are toothed, sharp pointed, and sometimes lobed. They are dark green and fuzzy on top, pale green and hairy underneath. When they emerge in spring, the leaves are grayish green; they turn red or yellow in fall. The inner scales of the winter buds are red at maturity. The ½-inch-wide, white to pink flowers have five petals similar to, but smaller than, those of commercial apple blossoms. The flowers are woolly inside and form fragrant, flat-topped clusters from April to June. The fruits resemble tiny apples but look more like berries because they are only ½ to ¾ inch across. They stay on the branches through winter.

Western crabapple inhabits coastal bogs, streambanks, and mountain slopes up to 2,500 feet elevation. It grows in coastal areas from Alaska to central California and is the only crabapple native to the western states.

Edibility: Crabapples are edible raw and good in jelly and sauce. They are much sweeter after the first frost. The seeds are high in cyanide and are poisonous if eaten in large quantities.

Historical Uses: Coastal tribes usually harvested crabapples after the first frost when they had turned soft, brown, and sweet. If picked green in late summer, they were stored in baskets, hung in cattail bags, or put in water inside cedar boxes until ripe. They keep well because of their acidity. Around 1900, a cedar box of crabapples was worth ten Hudson Bay blankets in trade.

Western crabapple was particularly useful in medicine. Coastal tribes commonly made a decoction from boiled bark and drank it for stomach upsets, ulcers, tuberculosis, and loss of appetite. They also used it as an eye wash. They carved such tools as adze handles, bows, wedges, and digging sticks from crabapple wood.

Wild Gardening: Western crabapple is drought tolerant, and the blossoms and fruit are attractive in a garden. Many horticultural varieties are available for USDA zones 4 to 6.

Western Crabapple flowers   *Malus fusca*

Western Crabapple fruit   *Malus fusca*

Indian Plum   *Oemleria cerasiformis*

Indian plum, the only species of *Oemleria*, is a deciduous shrub or small tree reaching 6 to 13 feet tall. It has a peculiar pungent odor and smooth, purplish bark. The alternate, nontoothed leaves tend to cluster and are somewhat lighter on the undersides. They are oblong, tapered at both ends, and 2 to 5 inches long. Before the leaves are fully developed, tiny, five-petaled, greenish white flowers bloom in drooping clusters 2 to 4 inches long. Male and female flowers are borne on separate plants. This harbinger of spring is one of the first shrubs to leaf out and bloom in coastal woods, conspicuously flowering from January to March. When the flowers are spent, clusters of ½-inch-diameter, dark blue fruits form, ripening by late summer.

Indian plum inhabits low elevations in moist areas west of the coastal ranges from British Columbia to central California.

Edibility: Indian plums are edible though the seed is large and the flesh thin. They are best when they have barely turned from red to purple, but if eaten too early, they are bitter and astringent. Keep a close watch as they ripen or the birds may get them first.

Historical Uses: Indian plum was never an important staple for Native Americans, though several Salish groups in the Northwest ate small quantities of fresh and dried plums. At large feasts, they mixed the fresh plums with oil because they were dry and hard to swallow. When preparing them for winter storage, the Indians packed the plums in hot oil. In northern California, the Shasta improved the taste by mixing them with wild currants. Apparently Indian plum was not a favorite with the Tolowa of California. They called it, "the wood that lies," perhaps because it blooms early in spring but doesn't set fruit for several months.

Native Americans prepared a medicinal poultice by chewing twigs of Indian plum and mixing them with fish oil. They made tea from the bark to use as a tonic, a laxative, and a remedy for tuberculosis.

Wild Gardening: Indian plum blooms when other plants are still dormant, adding interest to the winter landscape. Later in the season, the decorative bluish fruits call in the birds. We recommend Indian plum for moist coastal climates in USDA zone 6.

Indian Plum flowers
Oemleria cerasiformis

Indian Plum fruit
Oemleria cerasiformis

Cherries   *Prunus* species

Most cherries in the West are deciduous shrubs and bear fleshy to dry fruits with small stones. The small flowers have five petals and numerous stamens.

Chokecherry (*P. virginiana*) is usually less than 10 feet high but can reach 20 feet. The shrub has smooth, reddish gray bark with raised, horizontal slits—pores called lenticels—that are characteristic of *Prunus* species. The deciduous, 3- to 4-inch-long leaves grow alternately on the stem and are bright green with finely toothed margins. They are elliptical to oval, usually round at the base and pointed at the tip, and smooth or downy on the underside. The 4- to 6-inch-long racemes of tiny, white flowers cover the shrubs in May and June. Red to purple fruits are borne on short stalks along drooping spikes in August.

Chokecherry is at home in damp woods, stream borders, and dry hills below 8,200 feet. It grows in coniferous forests, rocky slopes, and oak-pine woodlands from southern California north through the coast ranges to British Columbia, in the Sierra Nevada, and in Washington, Idaho, and the Great Basin.

Bitter cherry (*P. emarginata*) has the typical reddish bark and finely toothed leaves of *Prunus* species. Unlike chokecherry, however, its leaves are usually rounded at the tips, and its white flowers usually bloom in round, flattish clusters. The red fruits are very bitter, berrylike drupes.

Bitter cherry grows on mountain slopes and streambanks from British Columbia south to California and east to Montana, Wyoming, Utah, and Arizona. In southern California it grows above 8,000 feet while in British Columbia it ranges down to sea level.

Desert Peach (*P. andersonii*) and **desert apricot (*P. fremontii*)** are similar shrubs with short, stiff, spiny branches. Desert peach has approximately 1-inch-long, elliptical leaves that are finely serrated and generally clustered. Its reddish pink flowers are usually solitary, and its reddish fruits are fuzzy like a peach. Desert apricot has roundish leaves, usually solitary white flowers, and yellowish fruit.

Desert peach grows at elevations of 3,500 to 7,500 feet along the eastern slopes of the Sierra Nevada and in the Great Basin. Desert apricot grows below 4,000 feet elevation in the Sonoran Desert and in Baja.

Redberry (*P. illicifolia*), also called islay or holly-leafed cherry, is a dense evergreen shrub. Its leaves vary from ¾ inch to 2 inches long, and their margins can be spiny or smooth. Small, white flowers bloom in 3-inch-long racemes in April and May. The ¾-inch-diameter fruits are red to bluish black.

Redberry is common on dry slopes and alluvial fans below 5,000 feet in the chaparral of the coast ranges of southern California.

Edibility: The fruits of all *Prunus* species are edible, but leaves and pits contain toxic hydrocyanic acid, so remove the pits before eating the fruit. Generation of Native Americans and pioneers have used chokecherries and related specie

Chokecherry flowers   *Prunus virginiana*

Chokecherry fruit   *Prunus virginiana*

for food and medicine with apparently no harmful effects. Chokecherries lose much of their tartness when very ripe and sweetened by the first frost.

 Leah's Chokecherry Jam, page 195

Historical Uses: *Prunus* species growing in the West played a vital role in the lives of many Native Americans. Though chokecherry is sweeter than bitter cherry and inhabits a larger region than desert peach, desert apricot, or redberry, all *Prunus* species were used where available. Chokecherry and bitter cherry were staple fruits that people ate fresh from the bush or dried for winter storage. Natives usually pulverized the cherries, including pits, molded them into cakes, and dried them in the sun to eat later with winter soups. They also mixed the fruit with meat for pemmican. Either the process of cooking and drying the cherries reduced the toxicity of the pits or the natives did not eat them in large enough quantity to become ill.

Many tribes prized the berries more for their seeds than for their fruit, though extracting the desirable kernel from the center of the pit was difficult. Usually, they squeezed the pits from the pulp, cracked them, and removed the kernels. The Chumash of California picked the berries, piled them up, and left them until the pulp rotted. The flesh then easily fell away, and the pits were ready to be dried and ground into a fine flour, which was later boiled for mush.

Native Americans and pioneers used *Prunus* species, particularly chokecherry and bitter cherry, extensively as medicines. They made a curative tea from a decoction of roots, bark, and leaves (which are toxic) and used it to treat colds, coughs, diarrhea, and stomachaches. Widely scattered Indian groups from the Navajo of Arizona to the Flathead of Montana and the Skagit of Washington placed their faith in this elixir. The Saanich of coastal Washington dosed their children with it to make them intelligent and obedient. Modern herbalists brew chokecherry bark for cough and cold treatments.

While crossing northern Idaho, Meriwether Lewis tried a chokecherry decoction. He had become ill with stomach pains and fever and decided to treat himself ". . . with some simples." He proceeded to boil a pot of chokecherry twigs until he had " . . . a strong black decoction of an astringent bitter taste." During the evening, Lewis nipped at this until he had taken about a quart. By bedtime the pain was gone. The next morning at sunrise, fit and refreshed, he is reported to have taken another swig of the remedy and resumed the journey.

Leaf poultices and preparations of powdered root were also used, usually as common cures for cuts and bruises. The Paiute mixed and boiled the bark and twigs to make an herbal steam for treating snow blind eyes. Bark was often dried and pulverized for smoking as a cure for headaches. Women commonly made a contraceptive from rotted cherry wood mixed with water.

The cherry wood had its own distinctive uses. Men crafted arrow shafts from straight cherry wood stems and also used the wood for prayer sticks and other ceremonial items. Sometimes Indians wore a cherry wood charm to ward off disease.

Throughout the West, Native Americans manufactured baskets and cordage from chokecherry bark. It was particularly useful for making imbricated designs in which materials overlap like shingles on a roof. Tribes also crafted dyes from chokecherry: the ripe, red fruits for red dye; green fruits for green dye; the roots for a dark brown dye; and the bark for a reddish brown dye.

Pioneer women cherished chokecherries, gathering them as eagerly as the native women did. Chokecherry jam was a favorite, and occasionally they turned the fruits into a festive red wine.

Wild Gardening: Because *Prunus* species offer a bonanza in spring flowers and fall fruit, they are a choice shrub for anyone interested in gardening with native plants. They grow in a variety of climates, from USDA zone 4 for chokecherry to USDA zone 8 for redberry.

Bitter Cherry flowers   *Prunus emarginata*

Wild Roses   *Rosa* species

Shrubs and vines of the *Rosa* genus usually have thorns and form thickets. The pinnately compound leaves have a terminal leaflet. The five-petaled flowers have twenty stamens and are often pink but sometimes white, yellow, or red. The fruit is the familiar rose hip, containing many seeds. The more than one hundred *Rosa* species grow in northern temperate regions and often hybridize.

Nootka rose *(R. nutkana)* is a 7-foot-tall bush with a pair of large thorns, straight or gradually curved downward, at the base of each leaf. The compound leaves have five to seven oval, toothed leaflets that are dark green above and fuzzy underneath. The showy, 2- to 4-inch-wide, pink flowers have distinctive, yellow centers and many stamens. The blossoms are usually solitary rather than clustered, and the petals are in a single layer. The ¾-inch-diameter fruits are smooth, reddish orange to purple rose hips that enclose many hard, white, hairy seeds. Rose hips overwinter on the bush.

Nootka rose inhabits moist or wooded areas from lowlands to mountain slopes. It grows in coastal areas from Alaska to northern California.

Wood's rose *(R. woodsii)* differs from Nootka rose in that the flowers are smaller and bloom in cymes rather than singly. Its fruits are also smaller, and its stems are gray or reddish brown.

Wood's rose grows in lowland creekside areas from the Cascade Range east to Wisconsin, Missouri, and Texas, and across Canada from British Columbia to Saskatchewan. Lewis and Clark discovered it near the mouth of the Niobrara River in South Dakota.

California rose *(R. californica)* is a 9-foot-tall bush with 2½-inch-wide, pink flowers that bloom in clusters of up to twenty. Its bent prickles are flattened. The flowers are paler pink than Nootka rose, and the hips have a distinct neck.

California rose grows in canyons and near streams below 6,000 feet elevation. It ranges from southern Oregon to southern California on the western side of the Sierra Nevada.

Baldhip rose *(R. gymnocarpa)*, unlike other wild roses, lacks green sepals at the top of the rose hips. It has slender, straight prickles, and the flowers are usually solitary.

It grows west of the Cascade Range from Washington to California, and also in northwestern Montana, northern Idaho, and northeastern Oregon.

Prickly rose *(R. acicularis)*, the emblem of Alberta, has 3-inch-wide flowers and double-toothed leaflets that look scalloped. The slender, straight prickles are scattered over the stems instead of only at the leaf nodes. The long sepals that linger on the hips resemble headdresses.

Prickly rose grows throughout Alaska and south through the Canadian Rockies to Idaho, Montana, Colorado, and New Mexico.

continued on page 146

Wood's Rose flower   *Rosa woodsii*

Edibility: Rose hips are dry and contain splinterlike hairs so they are not palatable until cooked and strained. The juice makes good jelly, and rose hip tea is rich in vitamin C. You can also eat rose petals, but they taste somewhat bitter.

 Zesty Rose Hip Syrup, *page 204*

Historical Uses: Some of the Puget Sound tribes ate rose hips, but others regarded them only as famine food. The reason, according to the Samish, was that the splintery hairs gave those who ate them "itchy bottoms." The thorns may have also deterred many harvesters. The name the Warm Springs tribes of Oregon gave the wild rose means, "mean old lady she sticks you."

Some tribes ate wild rose shoots in spring. In California, the Cahuilla picked rose buds and blossoms and soaked them in water to make a drink. The Washo made a rose-colored tea from the roots, and the Northern Paiute mixed the juice with browned flour to make a sauce or gravy.

Wild rose had many varied medicinal and household uses from warding off evil spirits to treating athlete's foot. The Paiute carried roses at funerals to keep the ghost of the dead person away. The Klallam chewed hips as a breath freshener, and the Quinault mixed rose twig ashes with skunk oil for an ointment to treat syphilis sores. Drinking an infusion of bark and rose hips was a general tonic and a common cure for arthritis, fevers, colds, and stomachaches. The Cheyenne drank a similar decoction for snow blindness, and the Chehalis women used a decoction of bark to ease childbirth. The Okanagan drank tea made from the branches to protect them from spells and evil spirits.

Native Americans used wild rose externally to soothe the skin and treat infections. They crushed dried petals for baby powder and mashed leaves into poultices for sore eyes, abscesses, and bee stings. The Paiute applied various parts of the plant, either dry or moistened, to cuts and burns. For athlete's foot, the Thompson scattered rose leaves in their moccasins.

Indians carved tools, arrow points, and fire-making drills from the wood of wild rose. In California, the Kawaiisu used wild rose stems for basket rims and fibers from the bark for cordage. The Indians of the Ute Mountain Reservation in southwestern Colorado made arrows from rose stems by pulling them through holes in pieces of bone to remove the bark and thorns.

Pioneers traditionally used rose hips for jelly and for medicine. People bandaged burns and wounds with rose petals and chewed petals for heartburn. They treated diarrhea with rose tea. Medicine made from the roots was given for diarrhea and for bleeding. In 1633 herbalist John Gerard listed more than two dozen medicinal uses for roses including strengthening the heart and refreshing the spirit. Today, oil of rose (or attar), distilled from the cultivated damask rose (*Rosa damascena*), is used in perfumes, lotions, soaps, and flavorings.

Wild Gardening: Wild roses are hardier and need less care than domestic roses, and birds relish the hips. Wild roses are usually available from specialized nurseries and are hardy in USDA zones 4 to 6.

Wood's Rose hips   *Rosa woodsii*

Blackberries and Raspberries   *Rubus* species

Rubus species often form tangled masses of thorny, trailing stems with which
berry pickers are well acquainted. In the West, the genus includes raspberries,
blackberries, salmonberry, and thimbleberry. The fruit is not a true berry but
an aggregate of drupes. There are more than two hundred species worldwide.

BLACKBERRIES

Pacific blackberry (*Rubus ursinus*), a native species,
is a clambering or mounding shrub with running stems
that root at the tips and with rather straight, bristly
prickles. The compound leaves are generally divided
into three elliptic to ovate leaflets that are irregularly
toothed and 1 to 4 inches long. The terminal leaflet is the
largest one. White flowers bloom in flat-topped clusters at
the branch tips. Male and female flowers are borne on separate
plants. Only the female plants bear fruit so it is possible to find
a large patch of blackberry plants with no berries. The fruit is an
oblong, purple to black berry about 1 inch long. Flowers and fruits form from
March to August.

Pacific blackberry is common in waste places, fields, canyons, and streamsides below 3,000 feet from British Columbia south to northern California and
east to Idaho.

Cutleaf blackberry (*R. laciniatus*) is a European evergreen bramble that
escaped cultivation. It forms dense thickets with long, arching stems. Its many
prickles have wide bases and are maliciously curved. The compound leaves
have three to five leaflets, each incised into narrow lobes or segments. The
flowers are mainly white to pinkish and almost 1 inch across. They develop
into a ¾-inch-long aggregate of drupes. The aggregate, or "berry," is shiny
black when ripe. It flowers and fruits from May to August.

Cutleaf blackberry has naturalized in northwestern California, the Sierra
Nevada, and on both sides of the Cascade Range north to British Columbia
and east into Idaho.

Himalayan blackberry (*R. discolor* or *R. procerus*) is very similar to
cutleaf blackberry except that it is not evergreen and does not have incised
leaflets. Himalayan blackberry, native to Eurasia, is widely naturalized west of
the Cascade Range from northern California to Washington and east into
northern Idaho.

Edibility: All blackberries are edible though they vary from juicy and delicious
to dry and seedy.

continued on page 15C

Cutleaf Blackberry fruit
Rubus laciniatus

Pacific Blackberry flowers
Rubus ursinus

Himalayan Blackberry flowers
Rubus discolor

Himalayan Blackberry fruit
Rubus discolor

Blackberry Cake, page 183
Dodie's Blackberry Sour Cream Mousse, page 187
Mixed Berry Salad Dressing, page 198
Mixed Berry Syrup, page 203

Historical Uses: Native Americans ate fresh blackberries, cooked them into sauces and jams, dried and stored them for winter use, or added them to pemmican. Tea made from blackberry leaves or roots was a universal treatment for diarrhea, stomach problems, sore throats, and mouth sores. Indians sometimes placed leaf poultices on wounds and snakebites. In areas where the blackberries were thick, one woman could gather 100 pounds of berries in an afternoon. A dense growth of brambles was a favorite hiding place for grizzly bears, so native women usually took dogs with them. If a grizzly appeared, the dogs would nip at its hind legs, distracting it while the women escaped.

Wild Gardening: Cutleaf blackberry and Himalayan blackberry form thick brambles that are difficult to control. We do not recommend introducing them to a garden as you may have to eradicate them later.

RASPBERRIES

Wild red raspberry (Rubus idaeus) is so much like the garden raspberry, it is like an old friend when encountered in the woods. The plants are spreading or erect, 3 to 4 feet tall, and covered with straight, slender prickles. The stems do not arch and root at the tips like blackberries but spread by means of creeping suckers. The compound leaves are divided into three to five leaflets, 1 to 3 inches long. Each leaflet has a rounded base, pointed tip, and sawtoothed edges. Small, ½-inch-wide, white flowers bloom in clusters in the upper leaf axils from May to July. In late summer the berries turn red (yellow on some plants) and ripen. The berry, a dense cluster of red drupelets, is about ½ inch across and usually matures from July to August. When picked, it is thimble shaped with a hollow center.

Wild red raspberry grows in moist places, open woods, and along streambanks at low to subalpine elevations. It is widespread, ranging from Canada south through Washington to northern California and in the northern Rocky Mountains.

Creeping raspberry (R. pedatus) is a trailing groundcover with stems that root at the nodes and have no thorns. Its compound leaves are usually divided into five leaflets, and the fruit resembles the red raspberry.

Creeping raspberry grows in moist areas from sea level to timberline. It ranges from Alaska south to the Cascade Range, northern Idaho, and eastern Montana.

Blackcap (*R. leucodermis*) is a raspberry-like bramble that is either erect or has long, arching branches that root at the tips. When young, the stems have a heavy, whitish bloom. Stout, curved prickles grow along the stems. The compound leaves are divided into three or sometimes five leaflets—two or four lateral leaflets and one large terminal leaflet. All are sharply toothed, up to 2 inches long, and have prickly veins. Each is rounded at the base, pointed at the tip, and has grayish, woolly hairs beneath. The small, white flowers bloom in compact, flat-topped clusters about ½ inch across. The ½-inch-diameter berries are purplish black, though sometimes reddish, and slightly flattened. They generally bloom and fruit from May to August.

Blackcaps grow on slopes and canyons below 7,000 feet in coniferous and mixed evergreen forests. They range from southern California north to British Columbia, and east to Montana, Idaho, Utah, and Wyoming.

Edibility: All raspberries are edible and vary in quality from dry to juicy and choice. Blackcaps range from sweet and juicy to bland and seedy. You can peel and eat the nutritious, young raspberry sprouts as a trail snack.

Lois's Raspberry Cheesecake, page 189
Raspberry-Strawberry Freezer Jam, page 196
Mixed Fruit Compote, page 198
Raspberry–Cottage Cheese Salad, page 199
Sweet Raspberry Vinegar, page 202
Mixed Berry Syrup, page 203

Historical Uses: Raspberries and blackcaps were a favorite food for Native Americans and pioneers. People ate them fresh, dried, mashed into flat cakes for drying, or in jam. Sometimes blackcaps were soaked in water to make a beverage. An infusion of leaves soothed the stomach and treated diarrhea and influenza. The Shoshone made a poultice of powdered blackcap stems to treat wounds and cuts. Modern herbalists make a raspberry leaf tea but advise using either very fresh or dried leaves as wilted ones may be mildly toxic. The fruit is a rich source of vitamin C, and the tender, young sprouts are nutritious.

Wild Red Raspberry fruit
Rubus idaeus

Blackcap immature fruit
Rubus leucodermis   **151**

Thimbleberry   *Rubus parviflorus*

Thimbleberry is an erect, many-stemmed shrub, growing 3 to 5 feet tall, and often forming thickets from its spreading rhizomes. You can easily distinguish it from other *Rubus* species by its large, maplelike leaves and thornless stems. The leaves grow alternately on the stem and are palmately divided, usually into five sharply pointed lobes with toothed margins. The leaves can be up to 6 inches across and are slightly fuzzy on both sides. The flowers are white and 1 inch or more in diameter, blooming in flat-topped clusters of three to seven at the branch tips. The berries turn from white to pink to red at maturity. Thimbleberry flowers and fruits from April to August.

Thimbleberries like shady streams, moist sites, open woods, and canyons below 8,000 feet. They grow in the Sierra Nevada and Cascade Range north to Alaska and east through the Rocky Mountain states.

Edibility: Thimbleberries are usually sweet and juicy but may be scarce as only a few mature at one time. They deteriorate quickly after picking.

 Thimbleberry Salad, page 199

Historical Uses: Native Americans ate thimbleberries wherever they were available. They liked the berries fresh or dried, cooked into a thick jam with wild raspberries, or soaked in water for a beverage. The big leaves were handy for lining cooking pits or berry baskets and for wrapping meat either to bake or to store. In spring, fresh shoots were peeled and eaten raw, steamed, or toasted. Thimbleberries were a useful addition to the medicine basket, too. A tea made from an infusion of roots was a blood tonic, a gynecological aid, and a treatment for stomach ailments.

Thimbleberry flowers   *Rubus parviflorus*

Thimbleberry fruit   *Rubus parviflorus*

Salmonberry
Rubus spectabilis

Salmonberry is a raspberry-like shrub that has light brown, shredding bark and few prickles. It grows from rhizomes and can be 9 feet tall, often forming dense thickets. Its dark green, compound leaves are composed of three sharply toothed leaflets. The beautiful, deep pink blossoms bloom in early spring. Deep-cupped berries develop in midsummer. They can be red, yellow, or salmon-colored.

Salmonberries are at home in damp woods, moist shady places, and streamsides. They grow from Idaho to Alaska, and south to California, mainly west of the Cascade Range.

Edibility: Salmonberries can be delicious but vary widely in taste and texture.

 Salmonberry–Cottage Cheese Salad, page 199

Historical Uses: Salmonberries as well as young stem sprouts were popular delicacies for most Native Americans in the coastal areas of the Pacific Northwest and northern California. They peeled and ate the raw sprouts for a juicy snack or steam-cooked them in a pit and served them with dried salmon. Salmonberry sprout feasts were common in spring. Participants would sing and dance on the beach while waiting for the sprouts to cook. When the salmonberries ripened in late summer, they were eaten fresh and dried.

Natives used decoctions of salmonberry bark and leaves to treat stomach problems, disinfect wounds, and decrease labor pains. They applied chewed leaves and bark to burns and toothaches. The Kwakuitl applied chewed sprouts to the head of a child to make the youngster grow.

Salmonberry flowers   *Rubus spectabilis*

Salmonberry fruit   *Rubus spectabilis*

Mountain Ashes   *Sorbus* species

Mountain ashes are deciduous shrubs or trees with compound leaves. The usually opposite leaflets grow along a central stalk. Flowers form a panicle and have five sepals, five petals, and fifteen to twenty stamens. The fruit is a pome. There are eighty *Sorbus* species, all in northern temperate regions around the world. The two species native to the West hybridize with each other and with the introduced European mountain ash (*S. aucuparia*).

Western mountain ash (*S. scopulina*) is a 20-foot-tall shrub with yellow or orange bark. It has pinnately compound leaves each with nine to seventeen shiny, dark green leaflets. The leaflets are opposite each other, 3 inches long, elliptical, sharply pointed, and sharply toothed. Their bases are rounded and asymmetrical. Young twigs are sticky and have white hairs. Fragrant, ⅜-inch-wide flowers bloom from May until August. Each cluster has fewer than twenty-five flowers. The orange to red, applelike berries ripen in September and stay on the tree into winter.

   Mountain ash grows in moist soils in open woods, thickets, and coniferous forests. It ranges from Alaska south to northern California and east to New Mexico, Utah, Idaho, the Dakotas, Wyoming, and Colorado.

Sitka mountain ash (*S. sitchensis*) differs from western mountain ash in having shorter, wider leaflets that are bluish green. They have rounded tips instead of pointed ones and are toothed only on the upper portions of the leaves. Young twigs and leaves have rust-colored hairs. Small, white flowers bloom in flat-topped clusters. The red berries have a whitish bloom and turn orange or purple at maturity.

   Sitka mountain ash is more common along the Pacific Coast from Alaska to northern California than it is inland.

Edibility: The mealy berries of western mountain ash are bitter but sweet enough to eat after the first fall frost. Sitka mountain ash berries are not palatable even after frost. Though the berries are edible, the seeds of both western species contain poisonous cyanide compounds.

Historical Uses: When food was short, some native peoples ate western mountain ash berries, often dried and ground into flour. They used ash berries more often in medicinal remedies. Most groups gargled an infusion of inner bark for sore throats and drank it for colds, flu, tuberculosis, and rheumatism. The We-suwet-en of British Columbia made what must have been a powerful brew of the bark of mountain ash, twinberry, and devil's club to relieve whooping cough. The Okanagan gave bark tea to their children to keep them from wetting the bed. To get rid of lice, the Bella Coola of British Columbia rubbed the berries in their hair. Pioneers used western mountain ash berries for pies, jam, jelly, and wine.

Wild Gardening: The handsome mountain ashes feature stunning clusters of white flowers and bright red berries. These trees endure cold, heat, and drought. Species and horticultural varieties are usually available for USDA zones 2 to 7.

Western Mountain
Ash flowers
Sorbus scopulina

Western Mountain
Ash fruit
Sorbus scopulina

SANDALWOOD FAMILY SANTALACEAE

The twenty-seven genera of this family of herbs, shrubs, and trees are semi-parasitic on the roots and stems of other plants. They have chlorophyll so they take only water and minerals from their host plants. Flowers have three to six tepals—a term used when the petals and sepals of a flower are identical. Stamens, which are usually attached at the top of the ovary, equal the tepals in number. The fruit is a drupe. Family members are mainly tropical and subtropical. *Santalum album* of India provides the commercial sandalwood and sandalwood oil.

Comandras *Comandra* species

Three *Comandra* species grow in America and one in Europe. The lower stems of the shrubs are woody, but the nonwoody upper stems die back in winter. The plants spread horizontally by rhizomes. Leaves are alternate, and the flowers are urn or bell shaped with a tuft of hair at the base of the anthers. The fruit is a drupe, with the flower remaining attached to it.

Bastard toadflax (C. umbellata) is the most common species of comandra in the West. Though it photosynthesizes, it parasitizes the roots of nearby plants. The three varieties of bastard toadflax—C. *umbellata*, var. *pallida*, C. *umbellata*, var. *californica*, and C. *umbellata* var. *umbellata*—are sometimes listed as separate species.

Bastard toadflax has pointed, narrowly elliptical leaves that look grayish green because of a whitish bloom. Whitish flowers arise in cymes near the top of the plant. They are bell shaped and have five (sometimes four) widely spreading sepals at the bottom of the bell. The stamens have a tuft of hair at the bases of the anthers. The blue, purple, or brownish drupes appear in August.

Bastard toadflax grows throughout much of North America. C. *umbellata* var. *pallida* grows in semiarid regions in dry to moist, well-drained soil from lowland to alpine elevations. It is particularly common in sagebrush communities. It ranges east of the Cascade Range in Washington and Oregon to Idaho and Montana. C. *umbellata* var. *californica* grows along the Pacific Coast.

Northern comandra (C. livida), a less common species than bastard toadflax, has oval leaves with rounded tips. Its small clusters of flowers look like miniature, greenish white stars. The ¼-inch-diameter berries are orange.

Northern comandra grows in northern Washington, northern Idaho, Canada, and Alaska. It prefers bogs and damp sites in open woods.

Edibility: Bastard toadflax concentrates selenium, which is poisonous, so do not eat the berries where it grows in selenium-rich soils. Elsewhere, the berries are edible. Northern comandra berries are much sweeter and tastier than those of the varieties of bastard toadflax.

Historical Uses: Native Americans ate the berries of bastard toadflax in times of food shortage. We have found no record of western Indians using northern comandra for food though they probably did so because the berries taste good. The Navajo used a decoction of bastard toadflax plant parts as a narcotic. They also used the decoction to bathe corns, eyes, and canker sores. In British Columbia, the Thompson mixed the roots of northern comandra with a woman's milk for an eye wash. The Arapaho made blue dye from a blue part of the roots.

Bastard Toadflax flowers   *Comandra umbellata*

Northern Comandra fruit
Comandra livida

SILKTASSEL FAMILY GARRYACEAE

The silktassel family has only one genus, Garrya.

Silktassels Garrya species

Garrya species are evergreen shrubs and trees from 3 to 20 feet tall. The opposite, simple, leathery leaves resemble manzanita leaves. Plants bloom in late winter and early spring, with flowers hanging in pendulous catkins. Male and female catkins grow on separate trees. The fruit is a berry that becomes dry and brittle when ripe. Identifying the various Garrya species is difficult. The differences between species are measured in the degree of hairiness of leaves and fruit, length of catkins, and variations in leaf margins.

Coast silktassel (G. elliptica) is an evergreen shrub or small tree that may grow 20 or more feet tall. Its leathery leaves are 1 to 3 inches long, elliptical, and woolly on the undersides. The margins are mainly wavy or rolled under. Tiny flowers form in silky, cream-colored racemes in late winter to early spring. The male catkins are 4 to 7 inches long, and the female catkins usually 3 to 4 inches long. Only the female flowers produce the chains of tiny, round, purplish fruits covered with whitish, feltlike hairs. Each fruit is a bitter, one-seeded drupe that matures in midsummer.

Coast silktassel grows on sea cliffs, dry slopes, and ridges below 2,000 feet. It inhabits chaparral or mixed evergreen forests throughout the coast ranges, the Sierra Nevada foothills, and western Oregon.

Fremont's silktassel (G. fremontii) has dark green, shiny leaves. The undersides are paler and slightly hairy but not woolly. Its leaves have smooth margins and turn yellowish green with age. The 2-inch-long, yellowish catkins are solitary or clustered and produce round, black to purple fruits.

Fremont's silktassel grows in the Sierra Nevada and in northern California through the coastal ranges to Washington. It also grows in the coastal mountains of extreme southern California.

Veatch's silktassel (G. veatchii) has leaves whose lower surfaces are covered with a woolly mat of dense, curly hairs. Its catkins are usually less than 2½ inches long, and the buff to purplish brown fruits are ovoid or round.

Veatch's silktassel likes dry slopes up to 7,000 feet elevation. It grows in southern California foothill woodlands, extending south to Baja and east to Utah and Arizona.

Edibility: The silktassel fruit is intensely bitter.

Historical Uses: Native Americans ate the bitter fruit only in times of hardship. Silktassels contain quinine, and several Native American groups used an infusion of inner bark to reduce fevers. They also brewed a leaf tea to treat stomach cramps, diarrhea, and colds. Modern herbalists use a silktassel leaf tincture by the drop as a muscle relaxer and pain reliever. They warn against using it for young children or during pregnancy.

Wild Gardening: The showy male catkins of silktassel start to bloom in December and hang on until midspring. Silktassels are hardy in USDA zones 6 to 8.

Coast Silktassel male flowers
Garrya elliptica

Coast Silktassel tree with
male flowers   *Garrya elliptica*

Coast Silktassel fruit on female tree   *Garrya elliptica*

SOAPBERRY FAMILY   SAPINDACEAE

Some 150 genera of the soapberry family are mainly confined to tropical and subtropical regions. Trees in this family are characterized by fleshy thick roots; pinnately compound leaves; and minute, unisexual flowers, which bloom in erect, branched clusters. The fruit is berrylike with amber or yellowish, translucent flesh.

Western Soapberry   *Sapindus saponaria var. drummondii*

Western soapberry can be a large, deciduous shrub or multitrunked tree usually growing 6 to 30 feet tall with a rounded crown. The reddish brown to gray bark is smooth or furrowed; twigs are yellowish green and downy with fine hairs. Each compound leaf is composed of eight to eighteen leaflets, growing in pairs. The leaflets are 2 to 4 inches long and ½ to ¾ inch wide, with smooth margins. In late spring, tiny, white or yellowish, fragrant flowers bloom in branched clusters 6 to 9 inches long and up to 2 inches in diameter. The ½-inch-diameter, amber-colored berries are nearly transparent. They mature in late summer and persist well into spring.

Western soapberry prefers clay soils or dry, limestone uplands in hills, valleys, grasslands, and oak woodlands at elevations from 2,500 to 6,000 feet. It grows in Arizona, southern New Mexico, Colorado, Texas, and Mexico and ranges east to Missouri and Louisiana.

Edibility: Soapberries contain **TOXIC** saponins and are not edible.

Historical Uses: Soapberries contain 37 percent saponin, a poisonous foam-producing chemical. In Mexico, people made a liquid soap from soapberries by mashing and straining them. It is reported to be particularly good for itchy scalp, though it may cause a skin rash on some people. Native Americans in the Southwest usually pounded yucca roots (*Yucca* species) to make soap rather than using soapberries.

Occasionally, southwestern Indians made a poultice of soapberry sap to apply to wounds. Modern herbalists believe tea made from the dried leaves makes an effective anti-inflammatory and analgesic.

Some Native Americans threw crushed berries in the water to stupify the fish they hoped to catch. They also made buttons and necklaces from the hard, dark soapberry seeds and arrows from the wood.

Wild Gardening: The western soapberry tree has distinctive multiple trunks and lingering, handsome clusters of amber-colored fruit. It is often cultivated in the Southwest and grows in USDA zones 6 to 8.

Western Soapberry fruit   *Sapindus saponaria* var. *drummondii*
—RICHARD PARKER PHOTO, PHOTO RESEARCHERS, INC.

SUMAC FAMILY
ANACARDIACEAE

The sumac family numbers as many as 70 genera and 850 species widely scattered throughout the warm regions of the world. *Rhus*, a common genus in the West, includes such useful plants as lemonadeberry, sugarbush, squawbush, and smooth sumac. Another genus, *Toxicodendron*, was formerly included in *Rhus* and contains the poison oaks and poison ivies. Sumac's milky or acrid sap accounts for the toxicity of some species. Other species have aromatic sap. This unlikely family also includes the cashew nut, the pistachio, and the mango.

Smooth Sumac
Rhus glabra

Smooth sumac is a straggling deciduous shrub, 3 to 8 feet tall, that often forms waist-high or head-high thickets from shallow, spreading roots. The alternate leaves are pinnately divided into eleven to thirty-one opposite leaflets that are lance shaped to narrowly oblong and 2 to 5 inches long. The bright green leaflets have a finely serrated edge and a whitish bloom on the underside. In fall they turn scarlet. Cream-colored flowers develop in late spring after the leaves appear, forming dense, pyramidal clusters up to 8 inches long. Equally dense clusters of ¼-inch-diameter, brick red drupes follow. The berrylike fruits are fuzzy.

Smooth sumac grows on dry slopes in plains and foothills throughout the West from southern British Columbia to New Mexico and east to the Atlantic Coast.

Edibility: All parts of smooth sumac are edible.

 Pink Lemonade, *page 179*

Historical Uses: Native Americans readily ate sumac berries either fresh, dried, or in a beverage that resembles pink lemonade. They also used smooth sumac as a medicine, often steeping leaves and bark to make a tea for skin rashes. They chewed a piece of root to relieve tongue and mouth sores. The Nespelem drained the milky latex from the stems to make a salve. Lewis and Clark observed that some of the Native Americans east of the Rockies added dried sumac leaves to their smoking mixtures.

To the natives, smooth sumac leaves turning scarlet in fall meant that the sockeye salmon were spawning.

Wild Gardening: Sumacs brighten the fall landscape with scarlet and orange foliage. Smooth sumac's spreading roots hold the soil in place on steep banks, forming colorful thickets. Many hardy cultivars are readily available and grow in USDA zones 3 to 6.

Smooth Sumac fruit   *Rhus glabra*

Sugarbush   *Rhus ovata*

This large, handsome shrub grows 4 to 10 feet tall and has shiny, evergreen leaves that are 1 to 3 inches long, with a rounded base and pointed tip. They are leathery with smooth margins and fold upward along the midrib. Elongated clusters of pinkish flowers cover the shrubs in March and April. Many tiny flowers that measure about ¼ inch in diameter form the dense 2-inch-wide cluster that appears at the branch tip. The berrylike, one-seeded drupes turn red and ripen in early summer. A sugary coating and short fuzzy hairs cover the slightly flattened, ¼-inch-diameter fruits.

Sugarbush likes dry slopes below 2,500 feet, mainly in chaparral and away from the coast in southern California and northern Mexico.

A close relative, **lemonadeberry (*R. integrifolia*),** often hybridizes with sugarbush. It also has oval, evergreen leaves, but they are flat rather than folded along the midrib, and margins are either smooth or toothed. The round, sugary, somewhat flattened, red drupes are approximately ½ inch in diameter. Lemonadeberry also grows at low elevations but prefers the ocean bluffs and coastal sage scrub of southern California and Baja.

Edibility: Sugarbush berries are edible, tasting something like Sweet-Tarts candy when fresh from the bush.

 Pink Lemonade, page 179

Historical Uses: Native Americans valued sugarbush for its sugar content. The Cahuilla and Digueño Indians of southern California treated coughs and colds with sugarbush or lemonadeberry leaf tea, a treatment similar to hot lemonade. Sometimes they chewed the fresh leaves to allay thirst while on a long trek.

Wild Gardening: The evergreen foliage of sugarbush shines in background plantings, and birds flock to the berries. Sugarbush grows well in USDA zones 7 and 8.

Sugarbush flowers   *Rhus ovata*

Sugarbush fruit   *Rhus ovata*

Squawbush   *Rhus trilobata*

Squawbush, a deciduous shrub, grows approximately 3 to 8 feet tall with a rounded crown. The densely growing branches turn down at the tips. Its compound leaves are composed of three slightly hairy leaflets that are 1 inch or less long and wedge shaped at the base. The terminal leaflet is larger than the two lateral leaflets. Occasionally the leaves are not compound but grow singly, with three lobes, as implied in the Latin name, *trilobata*. Small, dense clusters of yellow flowers form early in spring before the leaves appear. Sticky, red, berrylike drupes about ¼ inch in diameter contain a pit that surrounds the single seed.

Look carefully at squawbush when neither flower nor fruit is present because it looks suspiciously like poison oak (*Toxicodendron diversiloba*). Poison oak has three oaklike leaflets, irregularly lobed but larger and shinier than squawbush leaves. The uppermost leaflet of squawbush is larger, rounder, and more deeply lobed than that of poison oak. Poison oak and poison ivy bear small, greenish flowers and white fruit while squawbush has yellow flowers and red fruit. Squawbush leaves can also resemble those of golden currant (*Ribes aureum*). Squawbush inhabits open slopes, washes, shrublands, and rocky hillsides, usually at lower elevations. It is one of the most widespread sumacs in the West, growing in the foothills of the Sierra Nevada, in the Rocky Mountains from Idaho to New Mexico, and in Texas and Baja.

Edibility: Though not very toothsome, squawbush berries are edible.

Historical Uses: Native Americans sometimes ate the berries fresh but more often they dried and ground them into a meal, mixing it with ground corn. They also made a beverage that resembles pink lemonade. Tribes throughout the West made a leaf and seed decoction to treat such diverse ailments as colds, stomach problems, itch, and falling hair. Some groups mashed the leaves for body deodorant. They sprinkled the powdered berries on sores, and the Navajo made a squawbush lotion to treat poison ivy rash. They also used squawbush as a dye mordant, made a black dye from the leaves and roots, and fermented berries to produce an orangish red dye.

Southwestern Native Americans fashioned water bottles, sacks, sunshades, cradleboards, and winnowing baskets from the fibrous stems of squawbush. They preferred young shoots above all other materials for basketry.

Wild Gardening: The densely packed branches and compact shape of squawbush provides cover for wildlife and forms a useful landscape screen, even after the attractive, yellow leaves fall in autumn. The red berries attract birds. It grows in USDA zones 4 to 6.

Squawbush flowers
Rhus trilobata

Squawbush young fruit
Rhus trilobata —BOB MOSELEY PHOTO

Squawbush with last year's fruit and the current year's flowers
Rhus trilobata —BOB MOSELEY PHOTO

Poison Oak
Poison Ivy
Toxicodendron species

Formerly included in the *Rhus* genus, the six *Toxicodendron* species are native to North America and eastern Asia. These shrubs, trees, or vines have resinous compound leaves, either in threes or with leaflets along a central axis. Small flowers form in racemes, with male and female flowers on separate plants. The fruits are cream-colored to brown berries.

Poison oak and poison ivy contain oils with the chemical urushiol that produces an itching skin rash, swelling, and painful blisters. The oil looses its toxicity very slowly so anything that contacts the plants—shoes, clothes, or equipment—remains contaminated and can cause a rash on contact months later.

The best way to prevent the rash is to recognize the plants and avoid them. If, in spite of all precautions, you touch a plant, wash your skin thoroughly with lots of cold water. Warm water simply helps the oil penetrate the skin. When headed for the woods, add a tube of steroid gel to the first aid kit. If applied to the skin within the first twelve hours after contact, it may prevent the rash. Wash the skin before applying the gel. If a severe rash develops consult a doctor. Avoid the smoke from trash fires and brush fires where poison oak or ivy grows as it contains toxins that are harmful to the lungs.

Poison oak (*T. diversiloba*) is usually a 3- to 8-foot-tall, rounded or irregular bush, but it can also form a vine, clinging to trees and other shrubs by tiny, aerial rootlets that grow on its stems. Its compound, alternate leaves are composed of three leaflets, usually 1 to 3 inches long, with the terminal leaflet larger than the two opposite leaflets beneath it. The bright green, glossy leaves are oval and rounded or blunt at the tip. The margins are rarely smooth but are bluntly toothed, scalloped, or lobed. They turn a beautiful crimson early in the fall. Flowers are white or cream and appear sparsely in loose, drooping, lateral clusters. The fruits are whitish drupes about ⅛ inch in diameter.

Poison oak is common on wooded slopes, foothills, valleys, streambeds, and many other places from sea level to 5,000 feet. It grows mainly west of the Cascade Range from British Columbia south through Washington and Oregon, in the California coast ranges, and in the Columbia River Gorge. It occasionally follows streams east of the mountains into the shrub steppe.

Poison ivy (*T. rydbergii*), formerly called *Rhus radicans*, is a deciduous shrub often less than 2 feet tall though it can be nearly 5 feet tall. It spreads by creeping rhizomes, often forming a colony. It can also be a clambering plant, climbing up trees or bluffs or running along the ground but without aerial rootlets. Its alternate, compound leaves are divided into three oval leaflets, pointed at the tips and 1 to 3 inches long. The lower two opposite leaflets are usually smaller than the single terminal leaflet. Leaf margins are finely toothed or wavy. The glossy, bright green leaves turn scarlet in autumn. Tiny, cream-colored flowers grow in dense clusters from the leaf axils in May and June. Unlike those of poison oak, the clusters are upright rather than drooping. Each flower is less than ¼ inch in diameter and cup shaped, with five spreading petals. The white fruits are smooth, berrylike drupes about ¼ inch in diameter.

Poison ivy grows widely in the West along streambanks, bottomlands, and canyons, usually at elevations from 3,000 to 7,500 feet. You may encounter it in southwestern deserts along streams descending from the mountains. It grows from eastern Washington to Nova Scotia and southward and is particularly common in the Rocky Mountains.

Edibility: All parts of poison oak and poison ivy are **TOXIC** at all times, and you should avoid all contact with them.

Historical Uses: Some Native Americans may be immune to the toxin in poison oak and ivy. But whether the immunity is natural or induced by ingesting small doses of the plant over a period of time remains a mystery. Some southwestern tribes used these plants, treating warts and ringworm with the milky sap and applying a poultice of fresh leaves to rattlesnake bites. Sometimes they rubbed sap on freshly punctured skin to darken tattoos. A black dye compounded from the sap was used to color basketry materials. The Miwok in California spit on their skin to avoid a rash from poison oak. If they got a rash anyway, they bathed in Borax Lake or applied moss from the lake to the sores.

Poison Oak berries   *Toxicodendron diversiloba*

Sweet Gale Family   Myricaceae

The sweet gale family is composed of three genera and fifty species of shrubs and small trees with aromatic foliage. The leathery, simple leaves have toothed edges and no stipules. Resinous dots on the undersides of the leaves are aromatic. Male and female flowers form either on the same plant or on separate plants. The thin, greenish or yellowish blossoms have no calyx or corolla and form short spikes. Male flowers have from two to twenty stamens, and female flowers have one pistil. The fruit is a small nut or one-seeded berry.

Wax Myrtles and Bayberries   *Myrica* species

These shrubs or small trees have male and female flowers that may appear on different trees or on the same tree. The leaves are aromatic and toothed. The fruits are little spheres. Forty-eight species grow in temperate and subtropical regions. Do not confuse western bayberries with California bay, which belongs to the genus *Umbellularia* of the laurel family and is often called Oregon myrtle.

Wax myrtle (M. *californica*), an evergreen tree, usually grows no more than 20 feet tall though it can reach 60 feet and have a trunk 18 inches in diameter. Moss and lichens often cover the trunk. The smooth, thin bark is dark gray or light brown except on young branches where it is green and fuzzy. The 2- to 4-inch-long, alternate leaves are shiny, dark green, and finely serrated, with sharply acute tips. Black dots of resin on the underside smell pleasantly spicy. Tiny, yellowish male flowers grow in stalkless clusters in the leaf axils. The reddish green female flowers are bigger, up to ½ inch across, and higher on the tree. They bloom from March to May. Small, brownish purple berries, covered with lumps of white wax, mature from July to September.

Wax myrtle grows on hillsides in canyons and on stabilized sand dunes where it spreads out along the ground. It tolerates salt spray, growing along the Pacific Coast below 500 feet elevation from Puget Sound to southern California. You can see it near Florence, Oregon, and Ocean Shores, Washington.

Sweet gale (M. *gale*) is a low, deciduous shrub with alternate, narrow leaves that are broadest at the tips. The gland dots on the leaves are yellow instead of black. Nitrogen-fixing bacteria live on its roots. The flowers are borne in round or cylindrical clusters, male flowers on one plant and female on another. Both have no sepals or petals. The warty fruit is a minute, waxy berry dotted with orange resin glands.

Sweet gale lives in sphagnum bogs along the West Coast and in Alaska.

Sierra bay (M. *hartwegi*) is only 7 feet tall and has fuzzy, reddish brown twigs, deciduous leaves, and ⅛-inch-diameter nutlets covered with orange resin but no wax. Sierra bay grows in the northern and central Sierra Nevada foothills and ponderosa pine forests from 1,000 to 5,000 feet.

Edibility: Bayberry leaves and berries are **TOXIC**.

Bayberry Candles, *page 206*

Historical Uses: The Bella Coola of British Columbia made a decoction from the branches of sweet gale to treat gonorrhea and urinary problems. Settlers made tea from the bark, leaves, or roots and drank it for upper respiratory infections. Scientific studies show wax myrtle contains a substance that kills bacteria. Modern herbalists recommend a solution made from the root bark to heal inflamed gums and skin sores.

Early settlers used the bayberry wax for candles. To obtain the wax, they crushed the berries and dropped them into boiling water. Then they cooled the mixture until the wax solidified on the surface and could be lifted out. *Myrica pennsylvanica* and M. *cerifera*, eastern species, were the source of the wax used in bayberry candles of colonial times.

Wild Gardening: Wax myrtle is a delightful aromatic garden plant or hedge. You should be able to find it in a local nursery if you live anywhere in USDA zones 6 to 8.

Inset left:
Wax Myrtle berries
Myrica californica

Inset right:
Wax Myrtle flowers
Myrica californica

Bottom: Wax Myrtle with new vegetative growth   *Myrica californica*

YEW FAMILY

TAXACEAE

The yew family is composed of five genera and twenty species of evergreen trees or shrubs that are gymnosperms, plants that bear naked seeds. The leaves are flattened needles arranged alternately in two rows. Male pollen-bearing cones and female seeds are borne on separate plants. Female flowers develop a fleshy growth around the seed called an aril that looks like a berry.

Western Yew

Taxus brevifolia

Western yew can reach a height of 80 feet, though it usually forms small thickets. It has a straight trunk, drooping branches, and thin, fluted bark partly covered with reddish brown scales. The flattened, ¾-inch-long needles, similar to those of fir (*Abies* species), grow in two ranks along its green twigs. The shiny, yellowish green needles have soft, pointed tips and arch lengthwise with edges curved under. Two whitish bands of stomata line the undersides. Western yew is unusual for a conifer because it has no pitch.

In early spring, male trees produce cylindrical cones of yellowish pollen sacs. They arise in the axils of some needles just above a circle of bracts. Female trees produce minute, green flowers. In September and October, ⅜-inch-wide, fleshy, salmon to scarlet cups form on the female tree, each cup surrounding a large, brown seed. After pollination it takes two years for the seed to mature.

Western yew requires shade and prefers moist places in coniferous forests, particularly low-elevation streamsides in cool canyons. Though not common, it has a wide range, growing in southern Alaska, northern Idaho as far south as the Salmon River, the Santa Cruz Mountains of California, the western slope of the Sierra Nevada, western Montana, and the Selkirks of the Canadian Rockies.

Edibility: All parts of the western yew tree, except the fleshy cup, are **TOXIC**. The cup can be mildly toxic, and since the cups surround poisonous seeds, eating them is dangerous. The poison, an alkaloid, causes sudden heart failure by altering the rhythm of the heartbeat.

Historical Uses: The Haida of the Queen Charlotte Islands in British Columbia were one of the few tribes who dared to eat the red, fleshy cups. Several groups used the wood for tools and the needles for medicine. From the wood, they carved harpoons, bows, clubs, wedges, and digging sticks. They brewed tea from the needles, drinking small amounts to give them strength. They chewed the needles to put on wounds and dried the needles to smoke. Chemicals in the needles and twigs slow the heartbeat, so some tribes made a sedative from them. The Mendocino made poison. The Klallam boiled the needles and drank the liquid for pain.

The bark of western yew contains the complex chemical taxol, which is used to treat breast and ovarian cancer. The bark of ten trees was required to make enough taxol for one patient, so overharvesting threatened the tree with extinction. Now, pharmaceutical companies manufacture a semisynthetic form of the drug.

Western Yew berry   *Taxus brevifolia*

RECIPES

Beverages

Elderflower Tea
2 heaping teaspoons *Dried Petals* (see below)
1½ cups boiling water

Put dried petals into a small teapot. Cover with boiling water and steep for 5 minutes. Strain into a cup and drink hot. Add honey and lemon to taste. Garnish with a fresh mint leaf.

Dried Petals
Pick fresh elderberry flowers and dry them in a clean, brown bag for about 10 days or until they are dry and brittle. Store in small jar with tight-fitting lid. Be sure they are completely dry because any dampness left in the blossoms will cause mildew.

Mixed Berry Cooler
A beautifully colored and delicious drink

1 cup *Mixed Berry Syrup* (see recipe on page 203)
1 cup pineapple juice
2 cups water

Pour together and serve.

Mixed Berry Energizer
3 tablespoons *Mixed Berry Syrup* (see recipe on page 203)
1 ripe banana
⅔ cup skim milk or unsweetened yogurt

Whiz ingredients in blender. Serve in tall glass with mint leaf garnish.

Pink Lemonade

2 cups sugarbush berries or 8 cups dried sumac flower clusters
¾ cup sugar
water

Wash the fruits and cover with water in large kettle. If using dried sumac flowers, crush with a potato masher before soaking. Let fruit or flower clusters soak in the water for 30 minutes. Do not heat. Strain the juice through a jelly bag or cheesecloth. Add sugar and stir. Pour over ice. Add water to taste.

Breads

Blueberry Muffins

1¾ cups flour
⅔ cup sugar
2 teaspoons baking powder
¼ teaspoon salt
½ teaspoon baking soda
1 cup buttermilk
1 egg
¼ cup melted butter or vegetable oil
1 cup fresh washed and drained blueberries

Sift dry ingredients into mixing bowl and set aside. In separate bowl, beat eggs and buttermilk. Add butter or oil. Mix well. Combine the liquid and dry ingredients, stirring just enough to blend. Fold in blueberries. Fill well-greased muffin tins two-thirds full. Bake at 375 degrees for 20 to 25 minutes. While still warm, cover each muffin with a spoonful of Lemon Glaze (see next page).

Lemon Glaze

1 tablespoon unflavored gelatin
2 tablespoons cold water
½ cup boiling water
3 tablespoons lemon juice
2 cups powdered sugar
½ teaspoon cream of tartar

Dissolve gelatin in cold water. Boil ½ cup water and then add dissolved gelatin. Add lemon juice. Mix together sugar and cream of tartar and then add them to the hot liquid. Mix well. While still warm, spoon over muffins. The gelatin prevents the glaze from sinking into the muffin.

Nancy's Strawberry-Blueberry Muffins

**Recipe created by Nancy Pobanz,
well-known Oregon artist and gourmet cook**

1½ cups flour
¾ cup white sugar
½ teaspoon salt
2¼ teaspoons baking powder
3 tablespoons vegetable oil
1 egg, slightly beaten
3 tablespoons milk
¾ cup pureed strawberries
¾ cup whole blueberries

Sift the flour into a bowl and add sugar, salt, and baking powder. In a separate bowl combine the oil, egg, milk, and pureed strawberries. Make a well in the center of the flour mixture and add the liquid ingredients all at once. Stir only enough to moisten. Add blueberries. Stir briefly and ignore the lumps. Spoon batter into oiled muffin tins, two-thirds full. Bake at 400 degrees for 10 to 12 minutes.

Lowbush Cranberry (Lingonberry) Coffee Cake

1½ cups sifted flour
2 teaspoons baking powder
½ teaspoon baking soda
¼ teaspoon salt
½ cup sugar
¼ cup butter
2 eggs
1 tablespoon vanilla
1 cup cultured sour cream
1½ cups lowbush cranberries*, washed and drained

Mix Topping (see below) *and set aside. Sift and measure flour. Stir in baking powder, salt, and soda, and set aside. Cream butter and vanilla. Add sugar gradually to butter mixture and beat well. Beat eggs until fluffy and add to sugar mixture. Alternately add batter and sour cream to the dry ingredients. Fold together. Batter will be quite stiff. Turn batter into greased and lightly floured 9-inch-square pan (8-inch-square pan is too small). Scatter berries over the top of the batter. Sprinkle with topping and bake at 375 degrees for 30 minutes or until toothpick comes out clean. Serve warm or cold.*

* Blueberries may be substituted for lowbush cranberries. The coffeecake then resembles a blueberry buckle.

Topping
½ cup flour
½ cup sugar
¼ cup butter

Combine and mix with pastry blender until crumbly.

Serviceberry-Lemon Tea Bread

½ cup butter
1 cup sugar
2 eggs beaten
1⅔ cups flour
½ teaspoon salt
1 tablespoon baking powder
½ cup milk
1 teaspoon grated lemon rind
⅓ cup dried fruit
  (serviceberries, huckleberries, currants, or cranberries)

Cream butter and sugar. Add eggs and beat well. Mix dry ingredients and add to the batter alternately with the milk. Add grated lemon rind and fruit. Bake in greased 9-inch-by-5-inch-by-3-inch loaf pan at 350 degrees for 1 hour. While still hot, pierce bread several times with a toothpick and pour Topping (see below) *over warm bread. When cool, remove from pan. Bread tastes best if allowed to stand, wrapped in foil or plastic wrap, for 24 hours before cutting.*

Topping
¼ cup sugar
juice of 1 lemon

Combine and mix well.

Wild Strawberry Waffle Breakfast
An easy breakfast for company

1 quart vanilla yogurt
1 dozen frozen waffles
1 quart wild strawberries, sliced, with ½ cup sugar

Toast waffles in toaster and top each waffle with yogurt and strawberries.

Desserts

Blackberry Cake

2 cups sugar
3 cups flour
2 teaspoons baking soda
1/2 teaspoon cloves
1 teaspoon cinnamon

1/2 teaspoon nutmeg
1 cup egg substitute (or 4 eggs)
3/4 cup shortening
2 cups blackberries, cooked

Sift together dry ingredients. In a separate bowl, beat egg substitute and shortening until blended. Add blackberries. Mix with dry ingredients. Beat until well mixed. Bake in 10-inch-by-13-inch pan at 350 degrees for about 50 minutes, or until fork inserted in center comes out clean. Serve with whipped cream or ice cream, or frost with a vanilla or caramel frosting.

Blueberry Molasses Cake

This family recipe came to Margaret Fuller from her Grandmother Hanford. Auntie Morgan, the proprietress of a boardinghouse for young ladies in the 1890s in Middletown, New York, gave the recipe to Margaret's grandmother. In those days measurements were a little of this and a little of that. In the original recipe, ingredients were measured according to "the size of an egg." The modernized version follows:

1/2 cup sugar
1 1/2 cups flour
1 teaspoon baking soda
1/8 teaspoon salt
1 teaspoon cinnamon
1/2 teaspoon cloves

1 teaspoon ginger
1 large egg, beaten
3/4 cup molasses
5 tablespoons shortening
3/4 cup boiling water
1 cup blueberries

Sift the dry ingredients into a mixing bowl. Add beaten egg and molasses. Mix until flour disappears. Dissolve shortening in boiling water. Add to batter and mix well. Fold in blueberries. Pour into lightly greased and floured 8-inch-square cake pan and bake 40 minutes at 350 degrees.

Lowbush Cranberry (Lingonberry) Cake
An excellent Christmas gift

1 cup butter or margarine
1½ cups sugar
4 eggs
¼ cup milk
¼ cup orange juice
1 teaspoon grated orange peel
1 teaspoon vanilla

2¾ cups flour
2½ teaspoons baking powder
½ teaspoon salt
2½ cups berries
1½ cups walnuts

In mixing bowl, beat butter and sugar until creamy. Add eggs and beat well. In small bowl, combine milk, orange juice, orange peel, and vanilla. In a separate bowl, sift together flour, baking powder, and salt. Add dry ingredients to the butter and sugar mixture alternately with orange juice mixture. Mix until combined. Fold berries into the batter. Add walnuts. Pour batter into two greased loaf pans or one angel food cake pan and bake at 350 degrees for 1 hour or until fork comes out clean when inserted.

Mixed Berry Lemon Cake
1 box lemon cake mix,
    prepared and baked according to package directions
1 cup *Mixed Berry Syrup* (see recipe on page 203)
2 level tablespoons cornstarch
2 tablespoons water
whipped cream (optional)
½ cup chopped nuts (optional)

Mix cornstarch and water in a saucepan. Add mixed berry syrup and bring to a boil, stirring constantly. Reduce heat to simmer and cook until very thick. Remove from heat and cool. It will set up to a thick texture that spreads well and holds its shape.

Prepare cake according to package directions. When lemon cake is cool, spread berry filling between the layers, or if making a loaf cake spread filling on top and garnish with sweetened whipped cream and ½ cup chopped nuts.

Grandma Hanford's Currant Cookies

½ cup sour cream
½ cup butter
1 cup sugar
1 egg, beaten
1 teaspoon vanilla
¼ teaspoon nutmeg
1½ cups flour
½ teaspoon baking soda
½ cup dried currants

Beat sugar, sour cream, and butter until fluffy. Mix in beaten egg, nutmeg, and vanilla. Stir baking soda into flour and add to batter. Stir in currants. Drop by teaspoonful onto greased cookie sheet. Bake at 350 degrees for 12 to 15 minutes or until brown.

Mom's Serviceberry Squares

1 cup flour
1 teaspoon baking powder
¼ teaspoon salt
¼ teaspoon cinnamon
¼ cup butter
⅓ cup brown sugar
⅓ cup granulated sugar
1 egg
1 teaspoon vanilla
½ cup frozen serviceberries (do not thaw)
½ cup chopped walnuts

Mix flour, baking powder, salt, and cinnamon in bowl. Set aside. Melt butter in medium saucepan. Remove from heat. Beat in sugars, egg, and vanilla. Stir in flour mixture, then add serviceberries and nuts. Pour into greased 8-inch-square baking pan. Bake at 350 degrees for 30 minutes. Cool and cut into squares.

Huckleberry Pie

3 cups huckleberries
¼ cup water
1 cup sugar
3 tablespoons cornstarch

Mash berries, add water, and put in saucepan. Mix cornstarch with sugar and add to cold berries. Bring mixture to a boil and simmer 3 or 4 minutes until it thickens. Cool and pour into unbaked Pie Crust (see below). Add top crust and bake at 350 degrees for 50 minutes or until crust browns. Bottom crust will brown more readily if pie is put in cold oven.

Pie Crust

2 cups flour
½ teaspoon salt
⅔ cup vegetable oil
⅓ cup milk

Mix all ingredients and roll between 2 pieces of wax paper. Wipe the countertop with a wet cloth so wax paper will stay put. Sprinkle paper with thin film of flour. Divide dough and roll to thickness of ¼ inch and turn onto 8-inch pie pan. Use fresh waxed paper to roll second ball of dough for top crust. This makes plenty of dough for the pie with sometimes enough left over for jam tarts.

Cactus Candy

1 pound pulp of barrel cactus fruit
1 pound sugar
1 drop food coloring (optional)

Prepare the fruit by scooping the pulp out or by peeling away the thorny rind. Drain the pulp overnight to release its moisture. Cut into small pieces and boil with sugar until clear and tender, stirring constantly. Let cool, then boil again for about 30 minutes. Repeat until all liquid is absorbed. Pour into pan and cut candy into chunks while still warm.

Dodie's Blackberry Sour Cream Mousse

½ cup *Blackberry Juice* (see below) whipped cream (optional)
1 envelope unflavored gelatin sprig of fresh mint (optional)
½ cup cold water
½ cup boiling water
½ cup sugar
¾ cup sour cream
1 teaspoon vanilla

Soften gelatin in cold water. Bring the other ½ cup water to a boil. Turn heat off and add softened gelatin. Stir until it is dissolved. Add sugar and mix until dissolved. Pour ½ cup blackberry juice into gelatin mixture. Refrigerate until it begins to thicken, then fold in sour cream and vanilla.

Pour into parfait glasses and chill at least 3 hours. Garnish with a dollop of whipped cream and a sprig of fresh mint. The mousse can also be poured into a salad mold and used as a dinner salad.

Blackberry Juice

1 cup blackberries
¼ cup water

Wash berries and put them into a saucepan with ¼ cup water. Bring to a boil and simmer until berries are soft. Pour juice and pulp through a colander, sieve, or food mill to remove the seeds.

Buffaloberry-Apple Crisp

2 cups buffaloberries
    (use the berries of *Shepherdia argentea*, not *S. canadensis*)
2 cups diced cooking apples
⅔ cup sugar

Mix Topping (see next page) *and set aside. Mix washed whole berries and diced apples with ⅔ cup sugar and transfer to baking pan. Sprinkle with topping and bake at 350 degrees for 45 minutes, or until topping begins to brown and fruit is cooked. Serve warm with vanilla ice cream or frozen yogurt.*

Topping

²⁄₃ cup flour
½ cup sugar
¼ cup butter
¼ teaspoon cinnamon

Mix all ingredients with pastry blender until crumbly.

Huckleberry Bread Pudding

3 cups milk
3 cups white bread broken
    into 2- or 3-inch pieces
½ cup powdered milk
3 eggs

½ cup sugar
2 teaspoons vanilla
½ cup huckleberries
2 teaspoons sugar
nutmeg (optional)

Dissolve powdered milk in cold milk and heat. Pour into 3-quart casserole or baking pan and when cooled to lukewarm, add bread. Beat eggs slightly in bowl and add sugar and vanilla. Pour egg mixture into bread and milk mixture. Mash the huckleberries, heat in separate pan, and add 2 teaspoons sugar. Spoon this into bread mix. Stir only slightly to give a marbled effect. Sprinkle with nutmeg. Set baking dish in a larger pan of hot water. Bake at 350 degrees for 45 minutes, or until set. Serve with Lemon Sauce (see below).

Lemon Sauce

½ cup sugar
1 tablespoon cornstarch
1 cup water
3 tablespoons butter

½ teaspoon grated lemon rind
1½ tablespoons lemon juice
⅛ teaspoon salt

Mix sugar and cornstarch and add to 1 cup cold water. Mix well and pour into upper half of double boiler, or put the small saucepan in a slightly larger one that has about 2 inches of water in it. Boil, stirring cornstarch mixture until it thickens. Remove from heat and stir in butter, grated lemon rind, lemon juice, and salt.

Indian Ice Cream

½ cup soopolallie berries
½ cup water
2 tablespoons sugar

Mix berries and water in a grease-free (nonplastic) bowl. Beat mixture until it is the consistency of beaten egg whites, adding the sugar as the foam starts to form. If the berries are ripe, the foam will be pink. However, even with sugar added, it will still be sour and bitter. This dish is an acquired taste—it is so bitter you should test it before serving. To make it tastier, flavor with cinnamon and sugar, or try serving it over iced chocolate cake.

When picking soopolallie berries don't pick into a plastic bag or any other container that has a residue of grease or oil. Like egg whites, the mixture won't get stiff if any oil is present.

Lois's Raspberry Cheesecake

4 three-ounce packages cream cheese
2 eggs
¾ cup sugar
2 teaspoons vanilla

Mix and whip until smooth. Pour into Crust (see below) *and bake 15 to 20 minutes at 350 degrees. Pour Topping* (see next page) *over cheesecake and bake 10 minutes more. Chill cheesecake at least 5 hours. Top with Raspberry Sauce* (see next page) *before serving.*

Crust

12 graham crackers
¼ cup sugar
6 tablespoons melted butter

Crush crackers and mix with sugar. Melt butter and add to crackers. Mix together and press into pie plate.

Topping
1 cup sour cream
3 tablespoons sugar
1 teaspoon vanilla

Mix together.

Raspberry Sauce
5 cups raspberries, crushed
1½ cups sugar
¼ teaspoon salt
3 tablespoons cornstarch

Mix cornstarch with sugar and add to cold berries. Add salt and heat all ingredients to boiling. Simmer for 2 or 3 minutes until thick and clear. Remove from heat and refrigerate.

Meats and Vegetables

Saucy Cranberry-Elderberry Chicken
1 cup lowbush cranberries (lingonberries)
1 tablespoon *Elderberry Jelly* (see recipe on page 194)
¼ cup brown sugar
¼ teaspoon salt
¼ cup vinegar
3 tablespoons cornstarch
2 chicken breasts, split
2 tablespoons vegetable oil

Mix sugar, salt, vinegar, and cornstarch together. Heat cranberries with elderberry jelly over medium heat until jelly dissolves. Turn heat to low and add cornstarch mixture. Stir constantly until it begins to thicken. In a separate pan, brown chicken in vegetable oil. Place chicken in casserole dish and pour sauce over it. Bake covered for 45 minutes at 325 degrees. Uncover and bake an additional 10 minutes, basting frequently.

Groundcherry Crockpot Stew

1 pound stew beef, cut into bite-size pieces
5 large potatoes, peeled and cubed
1 large onion, chopped
3 stalks celery, chopped
3 large carrots, sliced
1 fourteen-ounce can diced or whole tomatoes
3 cups water
3 beef bouillon cubes
1 teaspoon pickling spice

8 gingersnap cookies, broken
2 cups frozen mixed vegetables (optional)
1 cup groundcherries, halved

Put first nine ingredients in crockpot. Cook on high for 8 hours. Then, add groundcherries, gingersnaps, and frozen mixed vegetables. Cook 1 hour more.

Lowbush Cranberry Stuffing

½ cup cooked fresh cranberries*   turkey or chicken gravy *or*
⅓ cup sugar   sauce made from
6 cups day-old bread   1½ cubes vegetable bouillon
1 cup celery, chopped   3 tablespoons flour
1 medium onion, chopped   pepper
4 tablespoons butter   Worcestershire sauce
1 teaspoon salt
2 teaspoons dried sage
     or ½ teaspoon each basil, thyme, and oregano

Cook cranberries until soft. Add sugar. Cool and place in large bowl. Cube bread or break into small pieces and add to bowl. Add chopped celery and onion. Melt butter and add salt and sage (or other herbs).

Pour over bread mixture and toss. Dressing should be light and slightly moist. Additional moisture is not necessary. Pour into baking pan and bake covered for 1 hour at 325 degrees.

Serve with turkey or chicken gravy. If gravy is not available, make sauce from vegetable bouillon. Add 1½ cubes bouillon to 1½ cups water. In a separate bowl, mix 3 level tablespoons flour with ½ cup cold water. Beat with wire whip until lumps disappear. Add to bouillon mixture and bring to a boil, stirring constantly. Turn to low and cook until thickened. Season with pepper and a few drops of Worcestershire sauce.

* You can substitute commercially grown cranberries for wild ones.

Bill's Juniper-Sauerkraut Casserole
A tasty vegetarian main dish

32-ounce jar sauerkraut
1 large onion, chopped
2 carrots, sliced
1 tablespoon vegetable oil
1 bay leaf
8 whole peppercorns
12 juniper berries
1 teaspoon dry parsley or 6 fresh sprigs
3 tablespoons soy-based bacon bits
2 vegetarian or chicken bouillon cubes
3 cups water
1 cup white wine

Drain sauerkraut and soak in water for 15 minutes. Change water and soak 15 minutes more. Drain sauerkraut in colander, squeezing out the water. Sauté onions and carrots in vegetable oil until onion is translucent. Stir in drained sauerkraut and simmer 10 minutes. Make a little bag of cheesecloth and put in parsley, bay leaf, peppercorns, and juniper berries. Place this bag and the sauerkraut mixture into a glass or ceramic casserole dish. Add bacon bits. Bring

3 cups water to a boil and add the bouillon cubes. When dissolved, pour over sauerkraut mixture. Add wine. Bake for 2 hours at 325 degrees, watching carefully that enough liquid remains so the sauerkraut doesn't burn. Remove spice bag before serving. Serves 6 to 8.

Juniper Chicken and Biscuits

1   cut-up fryer or 2 large chicken breasts
2   eleven-ounce cans cream of chicken soup
2   cups chicken broth
     (made by cooking chicken with juniper berries, see below)
1   ten-ounce package frozen string beans
5   large carrots, sliced
1   large onion, diced
10 juniper berries tied in cheesecloth bag
20 to 30 biscuits
     (make your own baking powder biscuits or buy packages of
       refrigerated biscuits from grocery store)

In a large pot, cover chicken and bag of juniper berries with 3$\frac{1}{2}$ cups water. Bring to a soft boil and immediately turn down to medium low and simmer for 1 hour. Remove chicken from broth and cool for 30 minutes. While chicken is cooling, add vegetables to the juniper chicken broth, leaving in the juniper bag, and cook over medium heat until vegetables are tender. Drain vegetables, reserving the broth. Remove the chicken from the bone and cut meat into small pieces. Mix the chicken soup with 2 cups broth and then add it to the chicken pieces, vegetables, juniper berry bag, and remainder of broth. Pour mixture into a flat pan and top with biscuits. Bake at 400 degrees for 30 minutes or until biscuits are brown.

Preserves

If you use powdered pectin, add the pectin to the fruit and bring it to a full boil before adding sugar. If you use liquid pectin, add the sugar to the fruit first and bring mixture to a boil before adding the liquid pectin.

For all jelly and jam recipes, use a large, heavy kettle with a thick bottom to boil the fruit. Stainless steel kettles work well. Do not use an aluminun pan.

Elderberry Jelly

3 1/2 cups elderberries
1/4 cup lemon juice
5 1/2 cups sugar
2 cups honey
1 three-ounce foil pouch of liquid pectin

Put elderberries in heavy, stainless steel kettle with 1/4 cup water. Mash berries and bring to a boil. Simmer until berries are soft. Strain through a colander or cheese cloth and add lemon juice. Add sugar and honey to elderberry and lemon juices and mix well. Bring to a boil, stirring constantly. When at a full rolling boil, stir in pectin. Boil for 1 minute. Remove from heat and skim off foam. Pour into hot sterilized jars and seal with sterilized canning lids.

Florence's Gooseberry-Currant Jam

4 cups gooseberries
2 cups red currants
1/2 cup water

4 cups sugar
2 tablespoons lemon juice
1 two-ounce box fruit pectin

Put berries, water, lemon juice, and pectin in a heavy, stainless steel kettle. Heat until boiling hard. Add sugar all at once. Bring to full rolling boil. Boil hard 1 minute, stirring constantly. Remove from heat and skim off foam. Fill hot sterilized jars and seal with sterilized canning lids.

Huckleberry Jam

4 cups huckleberries
½ cup water
¼ cup lemon juice

1 two-ounce package fruit pectin
6 cups sugar

Crush berries to release juices (potato masher makes it easy). Pour into a heavy, stainless steel kettle. Add water, lemon juice, and fruit pectin. Bring to a full boil, stirring constantly. Add sugar and boil hard for 2 minutes, stirring all the time. Skim and pour into hot, sterilized jars and seal with Kerr-type canning lids. Boiling an additional 2 minutes makes a stiffer jam.

Leah's Chokecherry Jam

2 quarts chokecherries
¼ cup lemon juice
apple juice as needed

1 package fruit pectin
4½ cups sugar

Simmer the chokecherries in a heavy, stainless steel kettle, adding ¼ cup water if necessary. When they are soft, press them through a strainer or colander to remove pits. This should make about 3 cups of pulp. If the measure is short, add apple juice to make 3 cups. Mix the pulp with lemon juice and 1 package of fruit pectin. Bring to a full rolling boil and add the sugar. Boil 1 minute after the mix again comes to a full boil. Remove from stove. Skim foam and pour into clean, sterilized jars and seal, or pour into plastic containers and freeze.

Oregon Grape Jelly

2½ cups Oregon grape berries
1 two-ounce package fruit pectin
2 cups apple juice

5 cups sugar
cinnamon (optional)

Wash berries and place in heavy, stainless steel kettle. Crush slightly and add apple juice. Bring mixture to a boil and simmer until fruit is soft (about 15 minutes). Drain in colander or through cheese-cloth. (Do not mash or squeeze.) There should be 3¾ cups of juice. Return to pan and add pectin. Bring to a rolling boil and add sugar. Boil hard for 2 minutes. Remove from heat and add a sprinkle of cinnamon. Skim off foam. Pour into hot sterilized jars and seal with sterilized Kerr-type canning lids.

Raspberry-Strawberry Freezer Jam

1½ cups mashed raspberries
1 cup mashed strawberries
4½ cups sugar
1 two-ounce box fruit pectin
¾ cup water

Wash three plastic, pint-size freezer containers and their lids. Make sure berries are at room temperature. Mash berries with a potato masher and measure. Stir sugar into crushed berries and let sit for at least 10 minutes. Put pectin and ¾ cup water in saucepan. Heat to boiling and boil 1 minute, stirring constantly. Add boiled mixture to berries and stir until no sugar crystals remain visible. Pour into containers. Let sit at room temperature for 24 hours so it will set. Store in freezer and thaw in refrigerator when ready to use.

Serviceberry Jam

3 cups serviceberries
 cup water
2 cups sugar
apple juice as needed
juice of 1 lemon
½ of a two-ounce package of fruit pectin

Put berries in heavy, stainless steel kettle, add water, and bring to a boil. Turn heat to low and cook until berries soften. Mash berries to release juice and put through a sieve or colander to strain seeds. Measure 3 cups of juice and pulp into kettle. If the measure is short, add apple juice to make 3 cups. Add lemon juice and pectin. Bring to a boil and add sugar. Boil 2 minutes. Skim and pour into clear plastic containers. When cool, place in the freezer. If glass jars are used they must be sterilized and sealed according to directions on the pectin package.

Wild Grape Jelly

4 cups wild grapes
1 cup water
apple juice as needed
5 cups sugar
1 two-ounce package fruit pectin

Clean and crush the grapes. Add water and simmer for about 20 minutes. Strain through a cheesecloth or fine sieve to remove seeds. Add apple juice, if necessary, to make 4 cups of liquid. Pour juice into a heavy, stainless steel kettle, add fruit pectin, and bring to a full boil, stirring constantly. Add sugar and continue stirring. Boil hard for 2 minutes. Remove from heat, skim, and pour into hot, sterilized jars. Seal with sterilized, Kerr-type canning lids, or pour into plastic canning containers and store in the freezer.

Salads and Salad Dressings

Lavender Blueberry Jello

1 large package (6 ounces) red jello
2 cups boiling water
1 medium can (20 ounces) crushed pineapple
2 cups mashed blueberries
1 cup cream, whipped
½ cup sugar

Mix jello and boiling water. Stir until completely dissolved. Chill until syrupy. Crush berries, saving a few for garnish. When jello begins to thicken add crushed berries and pineapple. Whip cream, adding sugar. Fold into fruit and jello mixture. Pour into clear glass dish or cake pan. Chill until set. Garnish with whipped cream and reserved berries.

Mixed Fruit Compote with Lemongrass Dressing

Chef Mary Joel Schaefer created this delicious dessert or luncheon salad, which comes to us through Idaho food writer Romaine Galey Hon.

2 cups blueberries
1 cup strawberries
1 cup raspberries
½ cup serviceberries

Make Lemongrass Dressing (see below) the day before. Wash berries and drain. Other berries and fruits of your choice may be used. Cut all fruit into small pieces except those like blueberries, which tend to bleed. Cut strawberries in half. Place fruit in bowl or individual compotes. Pour the lemongrass dressing over the fruit.

Lemongrass Dressing

8 lemongrass stalks, chopped
8 cups water
4¼ cups granulated sugar

In a saucepan bring the lemongrass, water, and sugar to a boil. Reduce the heat and simmer for 20 minutes. Remove from heat and set pan in ice water to cool. Cover and refrigerate overnight. The next day strain through a fine sieve and set aside until fruit compote is ready.

Mixed Berry Salad Dressing

Excellent tossed over crisped lettuce, broken walnuts, and celery slices

½ cup *Mixed Berry Syrup* (see recipe on page 203)
½ cup vegetable oil
¼ cup apple cider vinegar

Combine ingredients and pour into a small jar with lid. Shake well, but do not cook.

Raspberry (or Salmonberry) Cottage Cheese Salad

1 cup fresh wild raspberries or salmonberries
1 pint small curd cottage cheese
1/4 cup diced dried apricots
leaf lettuce
1/4 cup sliced almonds
2 tablespoons sesame seeds

Mix cottage cheese, berries, and apricots. Arrange on nest of leaf lettuce. Toast almonds and sesame seeds in oven or sauté them in oil until light brown. Sprinkle over salad.

Thimbleberry Salad

2 cups seedless grapes
1 sixteen-ounce can pineapple chunks, drained
1 cantaloupe, cut with melon baller
2 bananas, sliced
1 to 2 cups thimbleberries
1 cup undiluted, thawed orange juice concentrate

Mix all ingredients and serve. If orange juice concentrate is still partly frozen, allow it to thaw in the salad, but stir salad again before serving.

Wild Strawberry Shrimp Salad
A summertime dinner

1 six-ounce can tiny shrimp, drained and rinsed
2 large dill pickles, diced
2 stalks celery, diced
1 large cucumber, diced
1 cup fresh strawberries
2 tablespoons mayonnaise or more to taste
1 tablespoon vinegar
1 tablespoon sugar
lettuce

Mix mayonnaise, vinegar, and sugar and set aside for dressing. Combine remaining ingredients and arrange on nest of lettuce leaves on individual plates. Serve with French bread for dinner and have sherbet or watermelon for dessert.

Sauces, Syrups, and Condiments

Florence's Gooseberry Catsup
Excellent sauce for chicken or beef

3 cups gooseberries
1 cup crushed pineapple, unsweetened
1½ cups sugar
½ cup vinegar
½ teaspoon allspice

Mix all ingredients in a heavy, stainless steel kettle and bring to a boil. Simmer 1 hour or until thick enough to cling to a wooden spoon. Strain through a fine sieve. Seal at once in hot, sterilized jars or store indefinitely in the refrigerator.

Try this sauce on baked chicken breasts. Bake chicken until nearly done, then pour ½ cup gooseberry catsup over breasts and continue baking for an additional 15 minutes.

Groundcherry Chutney
Good with wild game, roast chicken, and bland vegetables such as squash

1 cup chopped onion
1 tablespoon butter
1½ cups groundcherries, cut in half
1 cup chopped apples
3 tablespoons brown sugar
2 tablespoons apple cider vinegar
1 teaspoon fresh grated ginger root
¼ teaspoon cinnamon
pinch each cloves and coriander
⅛ teaspoon nutmeg
1 tablespoon orange juice
1 tablespoon grated lemon peel

Sauté onion in butter until translucent. Add groundcherries and simmer 2 or 3 minutes. Add apples and simmer an additional 2 minutes. Apple bits should be tender but hold their shape.

Add brown sugar, vinegar, spices, and lemon peel. Stir well and remove from heat. Makes 1 pint. Seal in small, sterilized jars or store in the refrigerator for up to 2 weeks.

Huckleberry Sauce
Great on pancakes and heavenly on cheesecake

1 cup huckleberries
⅓ cup sugar
½ cup water
1 tablespoon cornstarch
2 tablespoons light corn syrup

Wash berries and place in saucepan. Mix cornstarch with water and add to cold berries. Add corn syrup. Bring to a boil, stirring constantly. Turn heat to low and simmer until thickened. Remove from heat.

Lycium Sauce
From *Edible and Useful Plants of California* by Charlotte B. Clarke. Published in 1978 by University of California Press, Berkeley. Reprinted by permission of the publisher.

1 onion, chopped
2 tablespoons butter, melted
2 teaspoons flour
2 cups fresh red berries
½ bay leaf
¼ teaspoon salt
dash black pepper
dash celery salt

Sauté onion in butter, add flour, and blend. Add berries and bay leaf. Cook 20 minutes. Remove bay leaf and add seasoning. Chill and use like catsup. Makes 1 cup. Add lemon juice or vinegar if you want a more tart sauce.

Salal-Pear Sauce

Excellent served warm over vanilla yogurt with a sprinkle of cinnamon

4 ripe Bartlett pears
1 tablespoon lemon juice
1 cup crushed salal berries
2 tablespoons honey
1¼ cups water

Peel, core, and dice pears. Mix pears, berries, water, and lemon juice. Cook until soft, stirring often. Add honey and mix thoroughly.

Salal Relish à la Pobanz

½ cup sugar
2 cups salal berries or blueberries
1 cup water
1 onion, very finely sliced
½ cup apple cider vinegar
1 clove garlic, crushed

In saucepan, combine sugar, salal, and water. Bring to boil over medium heat. Reduce heat and simmer about 10 minutes or until berries begin to soften. Remove from heat. Immediately stir in onion, vinegar, and garlic. Let sit 15 minutes to blend flavors. Serve warm or at room temperature. Will keep for 1 week, covered in refrigerator.

Sweet Raspberry Vinegar

1 cup sugar
½ cup water
1 cup wild raspberries
2 cups apple cider vinegar

Bring sugar and water to a boil. Add berries and simmer for a minute or two until the fruit is soft. Cool to lukewarm and add vinegar. Pour into covered container and refrigerate for 24 hours. Strain and pour into cruet or into bottle with acid-proof lid.

Mixed Berry Syrup

A wonderful syrup on pancakes, vanilla ice cream, or vanilla pudding. Use this versatile syrup in *Mixed Berry Cooler* (page 178), *Mixed Berry Energizer* (page 178), *Mixed Berry Lemon Cake* (page 184), and *Mixed Berry Salad Dressing* (page 198)

2 cups Mixed Berry Juice (see below)
1½ cups sugar
1 level tablespoon cornstarch

Mix the cornstarch with the sugar and add to cold, mixed berry juice. Put in medium pan, stirring constantly until mixture comes to a boil. Turn heat to medium and continue boiling for about 4 minutes. The mixture will thicken slightly as it cooks. Remove from heat. The syrup can be stored 2 weeks or more in the refrigerator.

Mixed Berry Juice

2 cups blackberries
½ cup raspberries
½ cup serviceberries
½ cup elderberries
½ cup water

Blackberries are basic to this syrup and in the absence of other berries can be used alone. Wash berries and place in large saucepan. Crush with a potato masher. Add water, cover the berries, and bring to a boil, stirring occasionally. Turn heat to low and cook for 5 minutes or until berries are soft. Put in colander or jelly bag to drain. (If there are more than 2 cups of juice, mix whatever is left over with white grape juice or apple juice for a delicious punch.)

Prickly Pear Syrup

From *Edible and Useful Plants of California* by Charlotte B. Clarke. Published in 1978 by University of California Press, Berkeley. Reprinted by permission of the publisher.

1 quart prickly pear fruits
water
2 tablespoons lemon juice
3/4 cup sugar
honey (optional)

Remove the spines and peel skin from the cactus fruits after boiling them a minute or two. Slice the fruit, discard any excess seeds, and add lemon juice and sugar to taste. Cook until mushy, drain off the juice, and strain it through a fine strainer. Add more sugar (or honey if desired) and cook it down to a syrup. Use in making punch, toppings, and pies. Makes 1 cup.

Zesty Rose Hip Syrup

4 cups rose hips
2 cups water
2 cups sugar
2 tablespoons lemon juice

Boil rose hips in water for 20 minutes. Crush berries and strain through jelly bag or cheesecloth to remove seeds, which have irritating hairs. Pour juice into a clean pan. Add sugar and lemon juice, and boil 3 to 4 minutes until syrup begins to thicken. Pour cooled syrup into a jar and refrigerate. The syrup will keep 2 weeks or more in the refrigerator. Use on pancakes or ice cream.

Variations: *While still hot, add cinnamon to taste or add 1/4 teaspoon powdered ginger or 1/2 teaspoon finely grated fresh ginger.*

Snacks

Berry Leather

3 cups crushed berries
¼ cup sugar

Mix and bring to a boil. Turn to low heat and stir constantly for 5 minutes. Run through a food mill or colander to remove seeds and make the mixture of uniform consistency. Pour onto greased cookie sheet that has a rim. Bake at 150 degrees until firm enough to peel off. This takes at least 5 hours. An alternate method is to cover the berry mixture with cheesecloth and dry in the sun for about 24 hours. When the mixture becomes leathery, roll it up and continue drying in a paper bag for a week. Cut into strips and store in an airtight container or it will continue drying and become too hard to chew easily.

Currant Granola

8 cups quick cooking rolled oats
1½ cups wheat germ
½ cup slivered almonds
½ cup dried currants
¾ cup honey
½ cup vegetable oil
2 teaspoons vanilla
1½ cups brown sugar
½ teaspoon salt

Mix oats, wheat germ, brown sugar, almonds, currants, and salt thoroughly in very large bowl. Heat the honey and vegetable oil in a pan over medium heat. When it bubbles, remove from heat and add vanilla. Slowly add the honey mixture to the oat mixture, stirring well. Spread the combined mixture over two greased, rimmed cookie sheets. Bake at 325 degrees for 20 minutes or until granola is just beginning to brown. Cool on cookie sheets, stirring occasionally to break up lumps. Store in large jar with lid or in plastic bags.

Spiced Pemmican

4 cups beef jerky, cut or broken into small pieces
4 cups serviceberries
3 tablespoons butter
3 tablespoons brown or white sugar
1/4 teaspoon powdered ginger
1/4 teaspoon cinnamon
1/4 teaspoon cloves

Mash serviceberries and mix with sugar, spices, and butter. Bring to a boil and simmer for 5 minues. When cool, mix with jerky and spread thinly in a baking pan. Dry overnight in oven at 150 degrees. You can vary the pemmican by adding unsalted nuts, sunflower seeds, or other berries. You may prefer it with more sugar than the recipe calls for.

Wild Crafts

Bayberry Candles
Softly green, aromatic, smokeless candles

1 gallon bayberries

Collect mature bayberries. These berries are poisonous to eat, so handle the berries and utensils with care. Crush berries and add to a large kettle of boiling water. The wax in the berries will melt at 120 to 130 degrees. Simmer for about 10 minutes, watching carefully to be sure there is enough water to prevent scorching. Remove from heat. As it cools (add ice cubes or refrigerate to speed the process), the wax will rise to the surface and harden. You can then lift it out. Reheat wax in a double boiler (it catches fire easily if heated in a single pan). Pour liquid wax into one large candle mold or several small ones that have been prepared with wicks. You may want to spread newspapers to catch spills because the wax is very difficult to remove from countertops and sinks. Take special care to keep it out of sink drains.

Lotion for Chapped Hands

¼ cup *Elderflower Water* (see below)
¼ cup glycerine
¼ cup witch hazel
1 tablespoon apricot oil
½ teaspoon borax
6 drops essential oil such as lavender or orange

Put all ingredients into a small, deep bowl and whip. When mixed, pour into a bottle and shake well. Lotion is ready to use. It will keep for about 3 months at room temperature and indefinitely in the refrigerator.

Elderflower Water

Use freshly picked elderberry flowers. Trim off the short stemlets. Measure 4 cups flowers into a small pan and add 1 cup boiling water. Stir quickly and cover. Let stand for 2 or 3 hours. Strain into a bowl and transfer to small containers.

Drying Berries

Dried berries are handy to have in the pantry as you can use them in place of raisins or currants in any recipe. Good berries for drying include serviceberries, huckleberries, blueberries, currants, and strawberries. Seedy fruits like blackberries and raspberries don't work as well. Elderberries should be cooked before drying as the raw berries may be toxic to some people. Strawberries should be halved first.

Wash the berries and place them in a colander or a cheesecloth bag. Dip berries (except for strawberries, which do not require blanching) in boiling water for one minute. Blanching promotes even drying. Otherwise the tough skin may dry, leaving the inside of the berry moist. After blanching, temporarily spread the berries on paper towels to dry, then place on screens covered with cheesecloth. Space the berries in a single layer and cover with another layer of cheesecloth.

Sun Drying

Dry berries outside in an airy place. They should dry in about 2 days. Check them often and turn them. When finished they should be leathery. Bring the berries in at night so they don't collect moisture. Do not dry berries outside in areas with air pollution.

Oven Drying

For oven drying, use the lowest temperature possible. Maximum temperature should be 140 degrees. Prop the oven door open half an inch or more to allow moisture to escape. Check frequently and expect them to become leathery in texture in about 8 hours or less.

Freezing Berries

Sweetened Berries

Wash and drain berries. Add 1 cup sugar for every 6 cups of fruit. Mix well and let stand 20 minutes. Put into plastic freezer containers with lids. Label each container with date and kind of berry. Store in freezer.

Whole Berries

Wash berries and soak up excess water with paper towels. Freeze spread out on cookie sheets in one layer. When frozen, put in plastic freezer bags and label with date and kind of berry. Store in freezer.

Selected Botanical Gardens

We found the following botanical gardens particularly helpful for plants that have berries.

Arboretum at Flagstaff
P.O. Box 670
Flagstaff, Arizona 86002

Boyce-Thompson Southwestern Arboretum
37615 U.S. 60
Superior, Arizona 85273

Tohono Chul Park
7366 N. Paseo del Norte
Tucson, Arizona 85704

Rancho Santa Ana Botanic Garden
1500 North College Avenue
Claremont, California 91711

Regional Parks Botanic Garden
Tilden Regional Park
Berkeley, California 94708

For information, contact:
East Bay Regional Park District
P.O. Box 5381
Oakland, California 94605-0381

Strybing Arboretum & Botanical Garden
9th Avenue & Lincoln Way
San Francisco, California 94122

University of California Botanical Garden
200 Centennial Drive
Berkeley, California 94720-5045

Mount Pisgah Arboretum
33735 Seavey Loop Road
Eugene, Oregon 97405

Plant Source Guide

Buffaloberry Farm
51 East Lakefork Road
McCall, Idaho 83638

Buffaloberry Farm is a relatively young nursery with a growing selection of desirable landscape plants. Many plants are custom grown for conservation projects.

Forest Farm
990 Tetherow Road
Williams, Oregon 97544

Offers a large selection of native berries and other native plants. All plants are propagated at the nursery; none are collected from the wild. A catalog to curl up with.

Goodwin Creek Gardens
P.O. Box 83
Williams, Oregon 97544

Enjoyable small catalog featuring native plants propagated at the nursery.

Arrowhead Alpines
P.O. Box 857
Fowlerville, Michigan 48836

Personable catalog that lists a few berries we have not found elsewhere. Their stock is nursery propagated or occasionally collected from the wild under State or Federal permit from land scheduled to be cleared.

Native Plant and Seed
400 East Butler Avenue
Flagstaff, Arizona 86001

They produce an informal newsletter with interesting information and plant lists.

Siskiyou Rare Plant Nursery
2825 Cummings Road
Medford, Oregon 97501

A great catalog for those interested in alpine plants and rock gardening. Most plants are propagated from nursery stock. They collect seeds from the wild but never take plants.

USDA
Plant Hardiness Zones

ZONE	AVERAGE ANNUAL MINIMUM TEMPERATURE IN FAHRENHEIT
2	-50 to -40
3	-40 to -30
4	-30 to -20
5	-20 to -10
6	-10 to 0
7	0 to 10
8	10 to 20
9	20 to 30

Geographic Glossary
of Native American Tribes

Tribes on the following list are limited to those we mention in the text.

Achomawi. Pit River area in northeastern California.

Apache. Plains of New Mexico and Texas.

Arapaho. Eastern Colorado and southeastern Wyoming.

Bella Coola. One of the northwest Salish tribes of British Columbia. Also called Nuxalt.

Blackfeet. Montana, Alberta, and Saskatchewan.

Cahuilla. Southern California in the areas of Palm Springs Canyon and the Sonoran Desert.

Carrier. Central British Columbia.

Chehalis. Southwestern Washington.

Cheyenne. East of the Rocky Mountains in Montana and Wyoming.

Chinook. Southwestern coast of Washington at the mouth of the Columbia River.

Chumash. A large California group, also known as the Santa Barbara Natives. They lived along the coast from San Luis Obispo to Malibu Canyon and inland as far as the San Joaquin Valley.

Coeur d'Alene. Northern Idaho near Lake Coeur d'Alene.

Comanche. Inhabited lands in southeastern New Mexico, Texas, and Kansas. Today, most of them are in Oklahoma.

Costanoan. Coast south of San Francisco Bay.

Cowlitz. South-central Washington.

Crow. Southeastern Montana and northern Wyoming.

Dakota. Largest division of the Sioux family, some of whom lived in Montana and Wyoming. Today, they have reservations in Montana and the Midwest.

Digueño. Southwestern coast of California and coastal Baja.

Flathead. Western Montana.

Gitksan. Northwestern coast of British Columbia.

Haida. Queen Charlotte Islands in coastal British Columbia.

Hoh. Western side of Olympic Peninsula in Washington.

Hopi. Northeastern Arizona.

Hupa (Hoopa). Northern California along the Trinity River. Today, the Hupa reservation is the largest in California and home to at least four groups including the Yurok.

*Geographic regions of Native American tribes
that are mentioned in* Wild Berries of the West.

Karok. Along the Klamath River in northern California.

Kawaiisu. Southeastern California from the San Joaquin Valley to the Mojave Desert.

Kiowa. Originally inhabited the head-waters region of the Missouri River in Montana but now live in northern Oklahoma.

Klallam. Northern Olympic Peninsula and southern Vancouver Island.

Kootenay (Kutenai). Northern Montana and Idaho.

Kwakuitl. Coast of southern British Columbia. Also called Oweekeno.

Maidu. Northern California in the Sacramento Valley and nearby Sierra Nevada.

Makah. Northwestern tip of Olympic Peninsula in Washington.

Mendocino. A small group within the Pomo culture in northern California.

Miwok. Central California on western slopes of the Sierra Nevada.

Modoc. Northern California near the Klamath River and into southern Oregon.

Navajo. A powerful tribe of New Mexico and Arizona.

Nespelem. Northeastern Washington.

Nez Perce. Northern Idaho and northeastern Oregon.

Nitinaht. Western Vancouver Island in British Columbia. Also called Ditidaht.

Northern Paiute. Southeastern Oregon, northern Nevada, and southwestern Idaho.

Nuxalt. Coastal British Columbia in the Bella Coola River valley. Also called Bella Coola.

Okanagan. Northeastern Washington and southern British Columbia. An interior Salish tribe.

Oweekeno. Coastal British Columbia. Alternate name for Kwakuitl.

Paiute. Southern Idaho, Utah, Nevada, Arizona, and California.

Papago. In deserts and arid lands of the Southwest, especially in southern Arizona. Today, a large number of them live in the Grand Canyon. Also called Tohono O'odham.

Pima. Around the Gila and Salt Rivers in southern Arizona.

Pomo. One of several distinct language groups with a similar culture. The best known Pomo group lived in northern California along the coast and in the Russian River valley.

Pueblo. Pueblo is a term used collectively for such people as the Zuni, Hopi, and Tewa.

Quileute. Southwestern coast of the Olympic Peninsula in Washington.

Quinault. Southwestern coast of the Olympic Peninsula in Washington.

Saanich. Southeastern Vancouver Island, British Columbia. A Coastal Salish tribe.

Salinan. A California linguistic family who lived in San Luis Obispo and Monterey Counties in California.

Salish (Salishan). A group of tribes, related by language, inhabiting coastal Washington and British Columbia. Includes the Coastal Salish, Straits Salish, Interior Salish, and Flathead of Montana.

Samish. Northwestern coast of Washington. A Salish tribe.

Sechelt. Coast of western British Columbia opposite Vancouver Island. A Salish tribe.

Shasta. Along the Klamath River in northern California and southern Oregon.

Shoshone. A large group living in southeastern Idaho, Wyoming, Nevada, and eastern California.

Shuswap. Southern interior plateau of British Columbia.

Skagit. Northwestern Washington, in the Skagit River valley and on Whidbey Island.

Skokomish. West-central side of Puget Sound.

Snohomish. Northeastern side of Puget Sound in Washington.

Squaxin. South of Puget Sound in Washington.

Swinomish. A small tribe of northwestern Washington.

Tewa. Northeastern New Mexico close to Santa Fe.

Thompson. Southern British Columbia.

Tohono O'odham. *See* Papago.

Tolowa. Northwestern California.

Tsimshian. North coastal region of British Columbia.

Ute. An important division of the Shoshonean tribes who lived in Colorado, Utah, and New Mexico. Today most of them live on a reservation in Colorado.

Warm Springs tribes. North-central Oregon.

Washo. Near Lake Tahoe on the California-Nevada border.

Wet-suwet-en. West-central British Columbia.

Yuki. In the Sacramento Valley and nearby Sierra Nevada.

Yurok. Northwestern coastal California in the redwood belt.

Zuni. Arizona and New Mexico.

Illustrated Glossary
of Plant Parts

Refer to the main glossary for definitions of terms.

Flower Arrangements

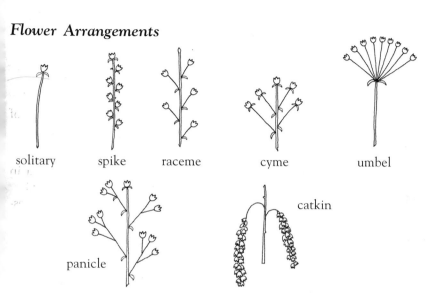

solitary   spike   raceme   cyme   umbel

panicle   catkin

Parts of a Flower

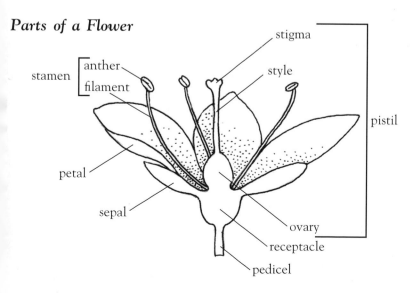

stigma

stamen — anther, filament

style

petal

pistil

sepal

ovary

receptacle

pedicel

Fruits

pome

drupe

berry

aggregate

Leaf Types

basal leaves at
base of stem

trifoliate

whorled leaves
attached at stem node

simple leaf clasping stem

COMPOUND LEAVES

pinnate

leaflet

leafstalk

palmate

Leaf Margins

entire

toothed

lobed

incised

Leaf Shapes

ovate

elliptic

lanceolate

Leaf Veins

pinnate

parallel

palmate

Glossary of Technical Terms

aggregate. Collected into dense clusters. A fruit formed by pistils clustering together, as in the blackberry.

alternate. Leaves or branches growing so they are not opposite or whorled along the stem.

annual. A plant that lives one year or season—from seed to maturity and death.

anther. The pollen bearing part of the stamen.

axil. The angle between the leaf and the stem.

basal. Situated at the base.

berry. A pulpy fruit developed from a single pistil, with no true stone, such as the blueberry

biennial. A plant that lives two years, usually flowering and producing fruit in the second year.

bloom. To produce flowers; also a fine, often waxy, powdery coating on the surface of certain fruits, leaves, or stems that makes them look whitish or bluish such as the bloom on a grape.

bract. A reduced or modified leaf from which an inflorescence or flower arises.

bristly. Bearing stiff hairs.

calyx. The outer ring of modified flower leaves, usually green, that enclose the flower. Individually these leaves are called sepals.

catkin. A spike or raceme bearing small flowers that lack petals.

clasping. A leaf that partly or wholly surrounds the stem.

compound. Composed of two or more similar parts joined together; a leaf with two or more separate leaflets; an inflorescence divided into smaller clusters.

corolla. All the petals of a flower.

creeping. Growing flat on the ground and rooting at the nodes.

crown. The part of a tree that bears the leaves.

cultivar. A cultivated variety of a species.

cyme. An inflorescence of several flowers of which the terminal flower on the main axis opens first, and the remaining flowers are borne on lateral shoots from the axils of leaves or bracts below.

deciduous. A plant that sheds its leaves annually.

decoction. A strong tea obtained by boiling plant parts in water for perhaps ten minutes.

downy. Closely covered with very short, weak, soft hairs.

drupe. A fleshy or pulpy one-seeded fruit with a hard stone containing the seed, such as a plum.

elliptic. Shaped like an oval, widest in the middle with rounded ends.

entire. A leaf margin that is smooth; not cut, toothed, or lobed.

evergreen. Bearing green leaves or needles throughout the year.

filament. The threadlike portion of a stamen.

fruit. The ripened pistil with all its accessory parts (ovary, style, stigma); the seed bearing structure of a plant.

gland. A tiny pit or knob, often on a leaf, that produces a sticky or oily substance.

habitat. The usual environment in which a plant lives.

herb. A plant that does not have woody stems and dies back to the ground at the end of the growing season.

host. A plant that nourishes a parasite.

hybrid. A plant resulting from cross-fertilization of one species with another.

incised. Leaf margin cut sharply and irregularly.

inflorescence. A flower cluster.

infusion. A light tea obtained by steeping plants in hot water.

lanceolate. Shaped like a lance: much longer than broad, widest in the middle, and tapering to both ends.

leaflet. The divisions of a compound leaf.

leafstalk. The stemlike part of a leaf that attaches the blade of a leaf to the plant stem.

lobed. Cut part way to the center with the outer parts rounded.

node. The place where a leaf or branch is attached.

opposite. Leaves growing directly across from each another at the same node; not alternate or whorled.

ovary. The structure of a plant that contains the ovules, which are undeveloped seeds.

ovate. A leaf shape broader at the stem end and tapering to the tip; shaped like a long section through a hen's egg.

palmate. Refers to a leaf divided into lobes diverging like fingers from the same point.

panicle. A branched flower cluster blooming from the bottom up.

parallel veins. Leaves with veins that form parallel lines.

parasite. A plant that gets its food and water chiefly from another plant to which it is attached.

pedicel. The stalk of a flower, whether growing singly or in a cluster.

perennial. A plant that grows for three years or more.

petal. Any member of the inside set of floral bracts in flowering plants. Many flowers do not have true petals.

photosynthesis. The process by which green plants produce their food (carbohydrates) from water, carbon dioxide, and minerals using the sun's energy.

pinnate. A compound leaf with the leaflets arranged on each side of a central axis.

pistil. The female organ of a flower composed of an ovary, stigma, and style (when present).

pollen. The male spores found in the anther.

pome. An applelike fruit with a core that contains the seeds.

pubescent. Covered with short, soft hairs.

raceme. An unbranched, elongated inflorescence with each pedicel having one flower fairly evenly spaced along the stalk; usually blooming from the bottom up.

receptacle. The structure to which flower parts or the entire flower are attached.

rhizome. An elongated underground stem or rootstock, distinguished from a root by the presence of nodes, buds, or scalelike leaves. Produces leafy shoots on the upper side and roots on the lower side.

riparian. Living alongside rivers or streams.

runner. A slender stem that grows along the surface of the ground and roots at its nodes or ends.

sepal. The outer circle of floral leaves found around the lower, outside edge of a flower, usually greenish and leafy.

serrate. Saw-toothed, having sharp, forward-pointing teeth.

shrub. A woody plant, usually low, that branches from the ground.

simple. A leaf that is undivided, unbranched, or single.

solitary. A flower appearing by itself rather than in a cluster.

spatulate. Shaped like a spatula or spoon, rounded at the tip and narrowed to the base.

spike. An elongated flower cluster whose flowers have no pedicels.

spine. A sharp-pointed, stiff, woody structure; usually the counterpart of a leaf.

stamen. A male or pollen producing organ in flowering plants; consisting of an anther (pollen capsule) and a stalk (filament).

stigma. The tip of the pistil on which the pollen lands and germinates.

stipule. One of a pair of leaflike structures attached at the base of the leafstalk.

stolon. A modified stem or runner usually rooting at the nodes or tips.

stomata. Tiny openings in the epidermis of plants, particularly the leaves, which take in oxygen and give off carbon dioxide and water vapor.

style. The stalk that connects the ovary and stigma.

tepal. One of a set of identical petals and sepals.

toothed. Having sharply pointed serrations.

trailing. Flat on the ground but not rooting.

tree. A large woody plant with a stem that is usually single for several feet above the ground.

trifoliate. Three leafed.

umbel. A flat or convex flower cluster in which three to many flower stalks radiate from a common point.

vein. A strand of conducting tubes that carry liquid through the leaf; a vascular bundle.

whorled. Three or more structures, such as leaves or flowers, radiating from a node.

Bibliography

Abrams, Leroy. 1923–1960. *Illustrated Flora of the Pacific States*, 4 Volumes. Vol. 4 co-authored by Roxana Stinchfield Ferris. Stanford, Ca: Stanford University Press.

Balls, Edward K. 1962. *Early Uses of California Plants*. Berkeley: University of California Press.

Barrows, David. 1900. *The Ethno-Botany of the Cahuilla Indians of Southern California*. Chicago: University of Chicago Press.

Benson, Lyman, and Robert Darrow. 1981. *Trees and Shrubs of the Southwestern Deserts*. Third edition, Revised. Tucson: University of Arizona Press.

Bowers, Janice E. 1993. *Shrubs and Trees of the Southwest Deserts*. Arizona: Southwest Parks and Monument Association.

Boyd, Robert. 1996. *People of the Dalles: The Indians of Wascopam Mission*. Lincoln: University of Nebraska.

Clarke, Charlotte B. 1978. *Edible and Useful Plants of California*. Berkeley: University of California Press.

Craighead, John, Frank Craighead, and Ray J. Davis. 1942. *A Field Guide to Rocky Mountain Wild Flowers*. Boston: Houghton Mifflin.

Crocket, Lawrence J. 1977. *Wildly Successful Plants*. New York: Macmillan Publishing Co., Inc.

Cutright, Paul Russell. 1969. *Lewis and Clark: Pioneering Naturalists*. Urbana: University of Illinois Press.

Davis, Ray J. 1952. *Flora of Idaho*. Provo, Utah: Brigham Young University Press.

Dunmire, William, and Gail Tierney. 1997. *Wild Plants and Native Peoples of the Four Corners*. Sante Fe: Museum of New Mexico.

———. 1995. *Wild Plants of the Pueblo Province*. Sante Fe: University of New Mexico.

Ebeling, Walter. 1986. *Handbook of Indian Foods and Fibers of Arid America*. Berkeley: University of California.

Elmore, Francis. 1944. *Ethnobotany of the Navajo*. Santa Fe: University of New Mexico.

Ford, Richard I., ed. 1986. *An Ethnobotany Source Book*. New York and London: Garland Publishing.

Foster, Steven, and James Duke. 1990. *A Field Guide to Medicinal Plants, Eastern and Central North America*. Boston: Houghton Mifflin.

Gerard, John. 1975. Reissue of 1633 edition. *The Herbal or General History of Plants*. New York: Dover Publications.

Gunther, Erna. 1945. *Ethnobotany of Western Washington*. Seattle: University of Washington.

Harbinger, L. J. 1964. *Importance of Food Plants in the Nez Perce Cultural Identity*. Pullman: Washington State University.

Hart, Jeff. 1992. *Montana—Native Plants and Early Peoples*. Helena: Montana Historical Society.

Hickman, J. C., ed. 1993. *The Jepson Manual: Higher Plants of California*. Berkeley: University of California Press.

Hicks, Sam. 1971. *Desert Plants and People*. San Antonio: The Naylor Company.

Hitchcock, C. Leo, and Arthur Cronquist. 1973. *Flora of the Pacific Northwest*. Seattle: University of Washington Press.

Horn, Elizabeth L. 1994. *Coastal Wildflowers of British Columbia and the Pacific Northwest*. Vancouver and Toronto: Whitecap Books Ltd.

Hunt, David, ed. n.d. *Native Indian, Wild Game, Fish & Wild Foods Cookbook*. Lancaster, Pennsylvania: Fox Chapel Publishing.

Hutchens, Alma R. 1992. *A Handbook of Native American Herbs*. Boston and London: Shambhola.

Karshaw, Linda, Andy MacKinnon, and Jim Pojar. 1998. *Plants of the Rocky Mountains*. Vancouver, B.C. and Renton, Wash.: Lone Pine Publishing.

Kearney, Thomas H., and Robert H. Peebles. 1960. *Arizona Flora*. Berkeley: University of California Press.

Kirk, Donald. 1970. *Wild Edible Plants of the Western United States*. Healdsburg, Calif.: Naturegraph.

Lampe, Kenneth F., and Mary Ann McCann, eds. 1985. *Handbook of Poisonous and Injurious Plants*. Chicago: American Medical Association.

Martineau, LaVan. 1992. *The Southern Paiutes: Legends, Lore, Language, and Lineage*. Las Vegas: K C Publications.

McKinney, Whitney. 1983. *A History of the Shoshone-Paiutes of Duck Valley*. Salt Lake City, Utah: Institute of the American West and Howe Bros.

Moerman, Daniel E. 1998. *Native American Ethnobotany*. Portland, Ore.: Timber Press.

————. 1986. *Medicinal Plants of Native Americans*. 2 vols. Ann Arbor: University of Michigan, Museum of Anthropology.

Moore, Michael. 1993. *Medicinal Plants of the Pacific West*. Santa Fe: Red Crane Books.

————. 1989. *Los Remedios: Traditional Herbal Remedies of the Southwest*. Santa Fe: Museum of New Mexico Press.

————. 1989. *Medicinal Plants of the Desert and Canyon West*. Santa Fe: Museum of New Mexico Press.

————. 1979. *Medicinal Plants of the Mountain West*. Santa Fe: Museum of New Mexico Press.

Moulton, Gary E., ed. 1988. *The Journals of the Lewis and Clark Expedition*. Vol. 5. Lincoln: University of Nebraska Press.

Mozingo, Daniel. 1987. *Shrubs of the Great Basin*. Las Vegas: University of Nevada Press.

Munz, Philip A. 1962. *California Desert Wildflowers*. Berkeley: University of California Press.

Munz, Philip A., and David D. Keck. 1965 and Supplement 1968. *A California Flora*. Berkeley: University of California Press.

Murphey, Edith Van Allen. 1959, reprinted 1990. *Indian Uses of Native Plants*. Glenwood, Illinois: Mendocino County Historical Society; Meyerbooks.

Nevada State Department of Education. 1967. *Uses of Native Plants by Nevada Indians*. Carson City, Nevada.

New York Botanical Garden. 1997. *Intermountain Flora: Vascular Plants of the Intermountain West*. Vols. 3 and 4. New York: Hafner Publishing.

Peattie, Donald Culross. 1981 edition. *A Natural History of Western Trees*. Boston: Houghton Mifflin.

Pojar, Jim, and Andy MacKinnon. 1994. *Plants of the Pacific Northwest Coast*. Renton, Wash.: Lone Pine Publishing.

Preston, Richard. 1968. *Rocky Mountain Trees*. New York: Dover Publications.

Robinson, Peggy. 1979. *Profiles of Northwest Plants: Food Uses, Medicinal Uses, Legends*. Second Edition. Portland, Ore.: Far West Book Service.

Rosenfeld, Lois G. 2001. *The Garden Tourist: A Guide to Gardens, Garden Tours, Shows, and Special Events*. Published annually by Garden Tourist Press in New York.

Ross-Collins, Margit. 1990. *The Flavors of Home: A Guide to Wild Edible Plants of the San Francisco Bay Area*. Berkeley: Heyday Books.

Scrimsher, Leda Scott. 1967. *Native Foods Used by the Nez Perce*. Moscow: University of Idaho. Reprinted 2001 by Boise State University.

Smith, Harlan. 1997. *Ethnobotany of the Gitksan Indians of British Columbia*. Hull, Quebec: Canadian Museum of Civilization.

Stevenson, Matilda. 1993. *The Zuni Indians and Their Uses of Native Plants*. New York: Dover Publications.

Storer, Tracy, and Robert Usinger. 1968. *Sierra Nevada Natural History*. Berkeley: University of California Press.

Strike, Sandra. 1994. *Ethnobotany of the California Indians: Aboriginal Uses of California's Indigenous Plants*. Germany: Koeltz Scientific Books.

Taylor, Ronald. 1992. *Sagebrush Country: A Wildflower Sanctuary*. Missoula, Mont.: Mountain Press.

Taylor, Ronald, and George Douglas. 1995. *Mountain Plants of the Pacific Northwest*. Missoula, Mont.: Mountain Press.

Thompson, Steven, and Mary Thompson. 1973. *Wild Food Plants of the Sierra*. Castro Valley, Calif.: Dragtooth Press.

Tilford, Gregory L. 1997. *Edible and Medicinal Plants of the West*. Missoula, Mont.: Mountain Press.

Townsend, John Kirk. 1970 reprint. *Journey across the Rocky Mountains to the Columbia River*. Fairfield, Wash.: Ye Galleon Press.

Train, Percy. 1957. *Medicinal Uses of Plants by Indian Tribes of Nevada*. Beltsville, Md.: U.S. Department of Agriculture, Plant Industry Station.

Turner, Nancy. 1997. *Food Plants of Interior First Peoples*. Vancouver: University of British Columbia Press.

———. 1995. *Food Plants of Coastal First Peoples*. Second Edition. Vancouver: University of British Columbia Press.

Underhill, J. E. 1980. *Northwestern Wild Berries*. Surrey, B.C.: Hancock House Publishers, Ltd.

U.S. Geological Survey. 1999. *Yucca Mountain as a Radioactive Waste Repository: A Report to the Director*. Washington, D.C.: U.S. Government Printing Office.

Vander Kloet, S. P. 1988. *The Genus Vaccinium in North America*. Ottawa: Canadian Government Publishing Centre.

Whiting, Alfred. 1939. *Ethnobotany of the Hopi*. Flagstaff: Northern Arizona Society of Science and Art.

Whitson, Tom D., ed. 1996. *Weeds of the West*. Fifth edition. Laramie: University of Wyoming, Western Society of Weed Science.

Recipe Index

bayberry candles, 206
beef, 191
beverages, 178–79
blackberries
    cake, 183
    mixed berry syrup, 203
    salad dressing, 198
    sour cream mousse, 187
blueberries. *See also* huckleberries
    buckle. *See* cranberry coffee cake
    jello, 197
    mixed fruit compote, 198
    molasses cake, 183
    muffins, 179
bread pudding, 188
breads, 179–82
buffaloberry-apple crisp, 187

cactus candy, 186
cakes
    blackberry, 183
    coffee, 181
    lowbush cranberry, 181, 184
    mixed berry lemon, 184
candles, 206
candy, 186
casseroles, 192
catsup, gooseberry, 200
cheesecake, 189
chicken, 190, 193
chokecherry jam, 195
chutney, groundcherry, 200
compote, mixed fruit, 198
condiments, 200–202
cookies, 185
crafts, 206–7
cranberries, lowbush
    cake, 184
    chicken, 190
    coffee cake, 181

    stuffing, 191
    tea bread, 182
crisp, buffaloberry-apple, 187
crusts, 186, 189
currants
    Grandma Hanford's cookies, 185
    granola, 205
    jam, 194
    tea bread, 182

desserts, 183–90
drying berries, 207–8

elderberries
    chicken, 190
    jelly, 194
    mixed berry syrup, 203
elderberry flowers, 178, 207

freezing berries, 208
frosting, 180

gooseberries
    catsup, 200
    jam, 194
granola, 205
grape jelly, 197
groundcherries
    chutney, 200
    stew, 191

huckleberries. *See also* blueberries
    bread pudding, 188
    jam, 195
    pie, 186
    sauce, 201
    tea bread, 182

ice cream, Indian, 189

jams, 194–96
jellies, 194–95, 197
jello, 197
juniper berries
    chicken and biscuits, 193
    sauerkraut casserole, 192

leather, fruit, 205
lemonade, 179
lemon glaze, 180, 188
lemongrass dressing, 198
lingonberry. *See* cranberries, lowbush
lotion, 207
lowbush cranberry. *See* cranberries, lowbush
Lycium sauce, 201

meat dishes, 190–93
mixed berry
    compote, 198
    cooler, 178
    energizer, 178
    lemon cake, 184
    salad dressing, 198
    syrup, 203
mousse, 187
muffins, 179–80

Oregon grape jelly, 195

pemmican, 205
pie, huckleberry, 186
preserves, 194–97
prickly pear syrup, 204

raspberries
    cheesecake, 189
    cottage cheese salad, 199
    freezer jam, 196
    mixed fruit compote, 198
    mixed berry syrup, 203
    sweet vinegar, 202

relish, salal, 202
rose hip syrup, 204

salad, 197, 199
salad dressing, 198
salal
    pear sauce, 202
    relish, 202
salmonberry–cottage cheese salad, 199
sauces, 200–202
serviceberries
    jam, 196
    lemon tea bread, 182
    mixed berry syrup, 203
    mixed fruit compote, 198
    Mom's squares, 185
    pemmican, 205
smoothie, 178
snacks, 205
soopolallie, 189
stew, 191
strawberries
    freezer jam, 196
    mixed fruit compote, 198
    muffins, 180
    shrimp salad, 199
    waffles, 182
stuffing, 191
sugarbush, 179
sumac lemonade, 179
syrups, 203–4

tea, 178
tea bread, 182
thimbleberry salad, 199

vegetable dishes, 190–93

General Index

Abies magnifica, 58
abrasions. *See* wounds
Achomawi tribe, 125
Acorus calamus, 40
Actaea rubra, 16–17
    pachypoda, 16
acupuncture, 14
alkaloids, 6, 32
allergic reaction, 44, 46, 60, 108, 162
Amelanchier species, 122–25
    alnifolia, 122–23
    florida, 122
    pallida, 124
    utahensis, 124
American ginseng, 40
Anacardiaceae, 164
analgesic, 8, 16, 41, 162
anticancer, 30
anti-inflammatory, 32, 162
antiseptic, 9, 14, 23, 41, 58, 98
antiviral, 30, 80
Apache tribe, 14, 30, 39
appetite, aperitif, 9; loss of, 69, 102, 136
apricot, desert, 140, 142
Aquifoliaceae, 72–73
Aralia species, 40–41, 100
    nudicaulis, 40–41
    californica, 40
    racemosa, 40
Araliaceae, 40
Arapaho tribe, 159
Arbutus species, 54–55
    menziesii, 54–55
    arizonica, 54
Arceuthobium species, 104–5
    campylopodum, 104
    tsugense, 104–5
    douglasii, 104
Arctostaphylos species, 56–59
    alpina, 56
    columbiana, 56
    glauca, 58
    nevadensis, 56–57

patula, 56, 58–59
    glandulosa, 56
    uva-ursi, 56–59
Arecaceae, 120
arthritis, 14, 42, 69, 80, 146
asparagus, 90–91
Asparagus officinalis, 90–91
astringent, 58, 59, 126, 134, 138, 142
athlete's foot, 146
baneberry, 16–17
    white, 16
barberry, 8
    Fremont's, 8
barberry family, 6
basketry, 9, 36, 52, 76, 80, 100, 108,
    121, 125, 143, 146, 168, 171
bastard toadflax, 158–59
bay, California, 88–89, 172
bay, Sierra, 172
bayberries, 172–73
bay tree, 88
beer, 40
bee stings, 146
Bella Coola tribe, 62, 92, 156, 173
Berberidaceae, 6
Berberis. See Mahonia
bite: insect, 106; scorpion, 9.
    See also snakebite
bittersweet, 114–15
blackberry, 148–50
    cutleaf, 148–50
    Himalayan, 148–50
    Pacific, 148–49
blackcap, 151
Blackfeet tribe, 16, 36, 59, 119, 124,
    128, 132
blister rust fungus, 51
blisters, 170. *See also* wounds
blood purifier, 8, 134
blueberry, 64–69. *See also* huckleberry
    Alaskan, 66
    oval-leafed, 66

boils, 16, 40, 42, 98, 128
boxthorns, 110
breath freshener, 146
bronchitis, 41
bruises, 80, 142
buckthorn, alderleaf, 10
buckthorn family, 10
buckthorns, 10
buffaloberry, 116, 118–19
    roundleaf, 118
bug repellant, 88
bunchberry, 32, 92
burns, 48, 59, 62, 76, 132, 146, 154
buttercup family, 16

Cactaceae, 18
cactus, 18–23
    barrel, 20–21
    beavertail, 22–23
    cholla, 22
    prickly pear, 22–23
    saguaro, 18–19
cactus family, 18
caffeine, 72
Cahuilla tribe, 58, 88, 111, 121, 146,
    166
Camassia quamash, 55, 128
Caprifoliaceae, 74
Carnegiea gigantea, 1819
Carrier tribe, 24, 119
cascara, 10, 12
Celtis species, 38–39
    reticulata, 38–39
    pallida, 38
ceremonial uses, 8, 30, 34, 36, 52, 59,
    132, 143
Chehalis tribe, 76, 146
Cherokee tribe, 72, 90
cherry, 140–43
    bitter, 140, 142–43
    holly-leafed, 140
chest cold. See expectorant
Cheyenne tribe, 16, 30, 59, 146
Chinook tribe, 68, 124
chokecherry, 140–43
Christmas berry, 134
Chumash tribe, 134, 142
cider, 55, 134
clintonia, red, 92
Clintonia species, 92–93
    andrewsiana, 92
    uniflora, 92–93

Coeur d'Alene tribe, 128
coffeeberry, California, 10–12
Comanche tribe, 14, 128
comandra, northern, 158–59
Comandra species, 158–59
    umbellata, 158–59
        var. californica, 158
        var. pallida, 158
        var. umbellata, 158
    livida, 158–59
Condalia lycioides. See Zizyphus obtusifolia
constipation, 46. See also laxative
Cornaceae, 32
Cornus species, 32–37
    canadensis, 32–33, 36
    nuttallii, 34–36
    sericea, 36–37
    stolonifera, 36
Costanoan tribe, 134
cough, whooping, 156
cough medicine, 16, 30, 32, 40, 42, 59,
    62, 98, 119, 142, 166
Cowlitz tribe, 92
crabapple, western, 136–37
cranberry, 70–71, 84–87
    Americanbush, 84–85, 87
    bog, 70–71
    lowbush, 70
    highbush, 84–87
Crataegus species, 126–29
    columbiana, 126, 129
    douglasii, 126–27
        var. erthropoda, 126
        var. suksdorfii, 126
    rivularis, 126
    suksdorfii, 126
Crow tribe, 42, 83, 119
crowberry, 24–25
crowberry family, 24
crucifixion family, 26
crucifixion thorn, 26–27
Cupressaceae, 28
currant, 44, 48–51, 138
    golden, 48–50, 168
    red-flowering, 48
    squaw, 48
    sticky, 48, 50
    stink, 48
    wax, 48–50
cuts, 23, 142, 146, 151. See also wounds
cypress family, 28

Dakota tribe, 39, 132
delphinium, 16
deodorant, 132, 168
devil's club, 42–43, 156
diabetes, 42, 59, 69
diarrhea, 46, 52, 62, 80, 96, 102, 119,
    128, 132, 142, 146, 150–51, 160
Digueño tribe, 132, 166
diuretic, 23, 30, 59
Disporum species, 94–95
    hookeri, 94–95
    smithii, 94
    trachycarpum, 94
dogwood, 34–37
    Pacific, 34–35
    red osier, 36–37
dogwood family, 32
doll's eyes. *See* baneberry
drought tolerant, 9, 30, 39, 83, 119, 136,
    156
dwarf mistletoe, 104–5; hosts, 104
    Douglas, 104
    western, 104
    western hemlock, 104–5
dye, 92, 168; black, 168, 172; blue, 159;
    brown, 39, 55, 119, 143; green, 30,
    80, 83, 143; purple, 80, 125; red, 39,
    143, 168; yellow, 9, 80
dysentery, 9, 86, 128

earache, 59, 88
Echinocactus acanthodes, 20–21
eczema, 132
Elaeagnaceae, 116
elderberry, 74, 78–81
    blue, 78–81
    desert, 78
    red, 78–81
Eleagnus commutata, 116
elk clover, 40
elm family, 38
emetic, 12, 16, 36, 50, 72, 82
emollient, 23
Empetraceae, 24
Empetrum nigrum, 24–25
Ericaceae, 54
Eskimos, 24
Exobasidium vaccinii, 64
expectorant, 42
eyewash, 9, 36, 50, 92, 94, 98, 136, 159

fairybell, 94–95
    rough-fruited, 94

fairy lantern, 94
false lily of the valley, 96–98
false Solomon's seal, 96–99
    star-flowered, 96, 99
fan palm, California, 120–21
Ferocactus cylindraceus, 20
fever, 9, 32, 34, 36, 42, 46, 60, 80, 83,
    108, 119, 146, 160
Flathead tribe, 8, 12, 59, 124, 142
Fragaria species, 130–33
    chiloensis, 130, 132
    vesca, 130–31
        var. *bracteata*, 130
        var. *crinita*, 130
    virginiana, 130, 133

gallstones, 9
gardening. *See* landscaping
Garrya species, 160–61
    elliptica, 160–61
    fremontii, 160
    veatchii, 160
Garryaceae, 160
Gaultheria species, 60–63
    hispidula, 60–61
    humifusa, 60
    ovatifolia, 60
    procumbens, 60
    shallon, 60–63
Gaylussacia species, 64
ginseng family, 40
Gitksan tribe, 132
gooseberry, 44–47, 50
    black, 44
    common, 44
    fuchsia-flowered, 46–47
    gummy, 46
    mountain, 46
    prickly, 44
    Sierra, 44–45
    swamp, 44–46
gooseberry family, 44
grape, 52–53
    California wild, 52–53
    desert, 52–53
grape family, 52
graythorn, 14–15
greenbriers, 100–101
Grossulariaceae, 44
groundcherry, 112–13
    lance-leafed, 112
    tomatillo, 112
    Wright's, 112
groundcover, 24, 32, 59–60, 150. *See also*
    landscaping

gynecological aids, 16, 30, 36, 46, 69, 83,
    125, 152; abortion, 30, 134; cancer,
    174; contraceptive, 30, 76, 98, 142;
    labor pains, 102, 119, 146, 154;
    muscle relaxation, 30; nursing, 16, 76;
    uterine tonic, 128, 132

hackberry, netleafed, 38–39
Haida tribe, 62, 98, 174
hawthorn, 126–29
    black, 126–27
    Columbia, 126, 129
    river, 126
    Suksdorf, 126
headaches, 12, 30, 32–33, 42, 59, 86,
    88, 142
heartburn, 146
heart disease, 128
heath family, 54, 84
hellebore, false, 96, 102
Heteromeles arbutifolia, 134–35
highbush cranberry, 74, 84–87, 98
Hoh tribe, 60
holly, 72–72
    California, 134
    English, 72–73
    yaupon, 72
holly family, 72
holly grape. *See* Oregon grape, creeping
hollywood, 134
Holocanatha emoryi, 26
honeysuckle, 74–77
    California, 74
    chaparral, 74
    double, 76
    northwest, 76–77
    orange, 76
    Utah, 74
Hopi tribe, 8, 111
huckleberry, 64–69. *See also* blueberry
    California, 64
    Cascade, 66
    evergreen, 64–65
    fool's, 64
    littleleaf, 66
    mountain, 64, 66
    red, 68–69
    western, 66–67
Hupa (Hoopa) tribe, 59

Ilex species, 72–73
    aquifolium, 72–73
    vomitoria, 72

immune system, 46, 171; white blood
    cells in, 41
Indian plum, 138–39
infections, 12, 42, 146; bladder, 55, 59,
    71; respiratory, 173; skin, 76; urinary,
    59, 62, 173
inflamed gums, 173
inflammations, 132
influenza, 12, 30, 80, 151, 156
islay, 140

jaundice, 9
Jefferson, Thomas, 82
juniper, 29–31
    alligator bark, 29
    California, 29
    common, 29, 31
    one-seed, 29, 106
    Rocky Mountain, 28, 31
    Sierra, 29
    Utah, 29, 106
    western, 29, 31
Juniperus species, 29–31
    californica, 29
    communis, 29, 31
    deppeana, 29
    monosperma, 29, 106
    occidentalis, 29, 31
    osteosperma, 29, 106
    scopulorum, 28, 31

Karok tribe, 9, 36, 55
Kawaiisu tribe, 98, 146
kidney: ailments, 8, 32; disease, 59, 72
kinnikinnick, 56–59
Kiowa, 50
Klallam tribe, 50, 62, 70, 94, 146, 174
Koeberliniaceae, 26
Koeberlinia spinosa, 26–27
Kootenay (Kutenai) tribe, 8, 58
Kwakuitl tribe, 40, 42, 50, 86, 154

landscaping: ornamentals, 12, 18, 52, 69, 76,
    84, 122, 125; screens, 52, 80, 168; shade-
    loving plants, 24, 40, 42; shade-tolerant
    plants, 16; windbreaks, 80, 119
Lauraceae, 88
laurel family, 88
Laurus nobilis, 88
laxative, 9, 12, 34, 36, 83, 108, 119, 138
lemonadeberry, 164, 166
Lewis & Clark, 6, 12, 34, 50, 54, 58, 74,
    76, 78, 83, 116, 122, 142, 144, 164

lice, 42, 156
Liliaceae, 90
lily family, 90
lingonberry. *See* cranberry, lowbush
liniment, 16
Lonicera species, 74–77
  ciliosa, 76–77
  conjugialis, 76
  hispidula, 74
  interrupta, 74
  involucrata, 74–75
  utahensis, 74–75
Loranthaceae, 104
Lycium species, 110–11
  andersonii, 110
  brevipes, 110–11
  pallidum, 110

madrone, 54–55
  Pacific, 54–55
  Arizona, 54
Mahonia species, 6–9
  aquifolium, 6–7
  fremontii, 8
  nervosa, 6–7
  repens, 8
Maianthemum species, 96–99
  dilatatum, 96–98
  racemosum, 96, 98
  stellatum, 96, 99
Maidu tribe, 30, 36, 76, 98, 114, 125, 134
Makah tribe, 32, 69–70, 83, 94, 102
malaria, 32
Malus fusca, 136–37
manzanita, 56–59, 160
  bearberry, 56
  pinemat, 56–57
  greenleaf, 56–59
  bigberry, 58
Mendocino tribe, 41, 88, 100, 174
Menziesia ferruginea, 64
mistletoe, 106–7; hosts, 106. *See also*
  dwarf mistletoe
  juniper, 106
  mesquite, 106–7
  oak, 106
mistletoe family, 104
Miwok tribe, 55, 58, 171
Modoc tribe, 76, 125
Moraceae, 108
Morus species, 108–9
  alba, 108–9
  microphylla, 108

mountain ash, 156–57
  European, 156
  Sitka, 156
  western, 156–57
Muir, John, 119
mulberry, 108–9
  western, 108
  white, 108–9
mulberry family, 108
muscle relaxer, 30, 160
Myrica species, 172–73
  californica, 172–73
  cerifera, 173
  gale, 172
  hartwegi, 172
  pennsylvanica, 173
Myricaceae, 172

narcotic, 159
Navajo tribe, 9, 30, 36, 39, 50, 83, 111–12,
  132, 142, 159, 168
Nespelem tribe, 36, 124, 164
Nez Perce tribe, 30, 50, 68, 83, 124, 126
nightshade, 114–15
  black, 114
  deadly, 114
nightshade family, 110
Nitinaht tribe, 42, 76, 94
Northern Paiute tribe, 146
Nuxalt tribe. *See* Bella Coola tribe

Oemleria cerasiformis, 138–39
Okanagan tribe, 36, 46, 102, 104, 126,
  146, 156
oleaster family, 116
Oplopanax horridum, 42–43
Opuntia species, 22–23
  basilaris, 22–23
  occidentalis, 22
Oregon grape, 6–9
  Cascade, 6–7
  creeping, 8
  tall, 6–8
Oregon myrtle, 88, 172. *See also* bay,
  California
Oweekeno. *See* Kwakuitl tribe

pain reliever, 41, 60, 134, 160, 174
paint: body, 52; face, 42; purple, 9, 76;
  black, 76
Paiute tribe, 8, 30, 50, 83, 98, 110, 142, 146
palm family, 120
palo blanco, 38

Panax cinquefolios, 40
Papago tribe, 18, 39, 108
Papaveraceae. *See* Koeberliniaceae
peach, desert, 140, 142
pemmican, 14, 50, 124, 126, 142, 150
Philadelphus lewisii, 122
Phoradendron species, 106–7
    californicum, 106–7
    flavescens, 106
    juniperinum, 106
Phyllodoce empetriformis, 24
Physalis species, 112–13
    ixocarpa, 112
    lanceifolia, 112
    virginiana, 112–13
    wrightii, 112
Pima tribe, 18–19, 39, 111
pleurisy, 40
poison oak, 12, 58, 168, 170–71
poison ivy, 36, 168, 170–71
Pomo tribe, 41, 55, 88, 124
porridge, 50, 121
poultice, 23, 40, 42, 50, 52, 62, 80, 83,
    88, 98, 114, 132, 138, 142, 146,
    150–51, 162, 171
prickly pear, 22–23
Prunus species, 140–43
    andersonii, 140, 142
    emarginata, 140, 142–43
    fremontii, 140, 142
    illicifolia, 140, 142–43
    virginiana, 140–43
Pueblo tribe, 30
purgative, 12, 16
Pyrola species. See *Gaultheria* species
Pyrus fusca, 136

queencup, 92–93
Quileute tribe, 32, 34, 60, 62
Quinault tribe, 16, 32, 70, 146
quinine, 32, 160

rabbitbush, 110–11
Ranunculaceae, 16
rashes: causes, 162, 170–71; cures, 12,
    36, 58–59, 164
raspberry, 150–51
    red, 150–51
    creeping, 150
redberry (*Rhamnus* species), 10, 13
redberry (*Prunus* species), 140, 142–43
Rhamnaceae, 10

Rhamnus species, 10–13
    alnifolia, 10
    californica, 10–11
    crocea, 10, 13
    purshiana, 10, 12–13
rheumatism, 9, 12, 60, 88, 90, 156
Rhus species, 164–70
    glabra, 164–65
    integrifolia, 166
    ovata, 166–67
    radicans. See *Toxicodendron rydbergii*
    trilobata, 168–69
Ribes species, 44–51
    aureum, 48–49, 168
    bracteosum, 48
    cereum, 48–49
    inerme, 44
    lobbii, 46
    lacustre, 44–46
    montigenum, 46
    roezlii, 44–45
    sanguineum, 48
    speciosum, 46–47
    viscosissimum, 48
rickets, 90
ringworm, 171
rope, 30, 36, 52
Rosa species, 144–47
    acicularis, 144
    californica, 144
    gymnocarpa, 144
    nutkana, 144
    woodsii, 144–45, 147
Rosaceae, 122
rose, 144–47
    baldhip, 144
    California, 144
    Nootka, 144
    prickly, 144
    Wood's, 144–45, 147
rose family, 122
Rubus species, 148–53
    discolor, 148–49
    idaeus, 150–51
    laciniatus, 148–49
    leucodermis, 151
    parviflorus, 152–53
    pedatus, 150
    procerus, 148
    spectabilis, 154–55
    ursinus, 148–49
Russian olive, 116

Saanich tribe, 142
saguaro. *See* cactus, saguaro
salal, 60, 62–63
Salinan tribe, 88
Salish (Salishan) tribe, 80, 83, 138
salmonberry, 148, 154–55
salve, 59, 164
Sambucus species, 74, 78–81
    cerulea, 78–81
    mexicana, 78
    racemosa, 78–81
Samish tribe, 50, 146
Sandalwood family, 158
Santalaceae, 158
Santalum album, 158
Sapindaceae, 162
Sapindus saponaria var. *drummondii*, 162–63
sarsaparilla, 40–41, 100
saskatoon, 122
scurvy, 24, 60
Sechelt tribe, 83
sedative, 174
serviceberry, 122–26
    Great basin, 124
    pale, 124–25
Shasta tribe, 138
Shepherdia species, 116–19
    argentea, 116, 118–19
    canadensis, 116–19
    rotundifolia, 118–19
Shoshone tribe, 8, 30, 83, 98, 124, 151
Shuswap tribe, 124
silktassel, 160–61
    coast, 160–61
    Fremont's, 160
    Veatch's, 160
silktassel family, 160
silkworm tree. *See* mulberry, white
silverberry, 116
sinus congestion, 30
Skagit tribe, 46, 142
Skokomish tribe, 132
Smilacina. See *Maianthemum*
Smilax species, 100–101
    californica, 100–101
    herbacea, 100–101
snakebite, 50, 52, 150, 171
Snohomish tribe, 16, 55
snowberry, 74, 82–83
    common, 82
    desert, 82
    mountain, 82–83
    trailing, 82–83

snowberry, creeping (*Gaultheria* species), 60–61
snow blindness, 124, 146
soap, 119, 162
soapberry (*Shepherdia* species), 116
soapberry, western, 162–63
soapberry family, 162
Solanaceae, 110
Solanum species, 114–15
    dulcamara, 114–15
    nigrum, 114
Solomon's seal. *See* false Solomon's seal
soopolallie, 116–19
Sorbus species, 156–57
    aucuparia, 156
    scopulina, 156–57
    sitchensis, 156
sores, 16, 41, 55, 59, 62, 80, 83, 106, 168, 171; canker, 159; mouth, 150, 164; skin, 9, 173; tongue, 164
sore throat, 46, 76, 80, 86, 150, 156
spikenard, 40–41
squashberry, 84
squawbush, 164, 168–69
Squaxin tribe, 83
steroids, 41, 170
stomach ailments, 55; ache, 60, 102, 104, 124, 132, 136, 142, 146, 150, 152, 154, 168; cramps, 54, 128, 160
Straits Salish tribe, 55
strawberry, 130–33
    woodland, 130–31
    mountain, 130, 133
    beach, 130
Streptopus species, 102–3
    amplexifolius, 102–3
    roseus, 102
sugarbush, 164, 166–67
sumac, smooth, 164–65
sumac family, 164
superstitions, 30, 98, 128, 154, 162; love potion, 94; luck, 9, 36, 50; warding off evil spirits, 30, 42, 59, 76, 83, 146
sweet gale, 172
sweet gale family, 172
Swinomish tribe, 76
Symphoricarpos species, 82–83
    albus, 82
    longiflorus, 82
    mollis, 82–83
    oreophilus, 82–83
syringa, 122

Taxaceae, 174
Taxus brevifolia, 174–75
Tewa tribe, 39
Thanksgiving cranberry, 84
thimbleberry, 148, 152–53
Thompson tribe, 50, 92, 102, 119, 124,
    132, 146, 159
thorn apple, 126
Tohono O'odham. *See* Papago
Tolowa tribe, 138
tonic, 8, 34, 36, 40–41, 59, 111, 138,
    146, 151
tools, 20, 30, 39, 55, 66, 68, 134, 146,
    174; arrows, 9, 36, 83, 125, 128, 134,
    142, 146, 162; armor, 125; bows, 9,
    108–9, 128, 136, 174; cordage, 121,
    143, 146; handles, 36, 39, 128, 136;
    harpoons, 174; nets, 121; rakes, 128;
    spears, 125; wedges,136, 174
toothache, 50, 88, 111, 154
Toxicodendron species, 164, 170–71
    diversiloba, 168, 170–71
    rydbergii, 170–71
toyon, 134–35
Tsimshian tribe, 64
tuberculosis, 40, 42, 46, 62, 119, 136,
    138, 156
twinberry, 74–75, 156
    black, 74–75
    red, 74–75
twisted stalk, 102–3
    rosy, 102

ulcers, 136
Ulmus, 38
Umbellularia californica, 88–89, 172
Ute tribe, 146
Uva corinthiaca, 44

Vaccinium species, 64–71
    alaskaense, 66
    deliciosum, 66
    macrocarpon, 70
    membranaceum, 64, 66
    occidentale, 66–67
    ovalifolium, 66
    ovatum, 64–65
    oxycoccus, 70–71
    parvifolium, 68–69
    scoparium, 66–67
    vitis-idaea, 70

venereal diseases, 46, 128; gonorrhea, 42,
    59, 119, 173; syphilis, 142
Veratrum viride, 96, 102
viburnum, oval-leafed, 84–85
Viburnum species, 84–87
    edule, 84
    ellipticum, 84–85
    opulus var. *americanum*, 84
    trilobum, 84–85, 87
Vitaceae, 52
Vitis species, 52–53
    californica, 53–53
    girdiana, 52–53
    vinifera, 52

Warm Springs tribe, 146
warts, 12, 83, 106, 171
Washingtonia filifera, 120–21
Washo tribe, 146
waxberry. *See* snowberries
wax myrtle, 172–73
weapons. *See* tools
weaving, 76
Wet-suwet-en tribe, 156
whortleberry, 64
    grouse, 66–67
wine, 40, 58, 62
wintergreen, 60–61, 92
    alpine, 60
    slender, 60
witches' broom. *See* dwarf mistletoe
wolfberry, 110
    Anderson's, 110
    pale, 110
wounds, 9, 23, 48, 55, 59, 62, 76, 80, 83,
    92–94, 98, 111, 134, 150–51, 154,
    162, 174

xeriscaping, 23

yew, western, 174–75
yew family, 174
Yucca species, 162
    brevifolia, 58
Yuki tribe, 30, 55
Yurok tribe, 55

Zizyphus obtusifolia, 14–15
Zuni tribe, 30, 111, 112

About the Authors

Betty B. Derig has a master's in U.S. history from the University of Montana. She has written numerous articles and four books on western history, including *Roadside History of Idaho* (ISBN 0-87842-328-1). Derig, an avid gardener, is a member of the Idaho Native Plant Society. Her love for the West's varied terrain, from its deserts to its evergreen forests, led her to team up with a natural history buff to write this book. Both authors reside in Weiser, Idaho.

Margaret C. Fuller has a biology degree from Stanford University and is a freelance writer. She is the author of six books and numerous articles on outdoor activities and mountain ecology. A seasoned hiker and photographer, she has logged more than 5,000 miles of trail, presented more than 200 slide shows, and taught workshops on backpacking and ecology.

We encourage you to patronize your local bookstores. Most stores will order any title that they do not stock. You may also order directly from Mountain Press by mail, using the order form provided below or by calling our toll-free number and using your VISA, MasterCard, Discover, or American Express. We will gladly send you a complete catalog upon request.

Some other Natural History titles of interest:

____Alpine Wildflowers of the Rocky Mountains	$14.00
____Birds of the Central Rockies	$14.00
____Birds of the Northern Rockies	$12.00
____Birds of the Pacific Northwest Mountains	$14.00
____Coastal Wildflowers of the Pacific Northwest	$14.00
____Desert Wildflowers of North America	$24.00
____Edible and Medicinal Plants of the West	$21.00
____From Earth to Herbalist An Earth-Conscious Guide to Medicinal Plants	$21.00
____A Guide to Rock Art Sites Southern California and Southern Nevada	$20.00
____An Introduction to Northern California Birds	$14.00
____An Introduction to Southern California Birds	$14.00
____The Lochsa Story Land Ethics in the Bitterroot Mountains	$20.00
____Mountain Plants of the Pacific Northwest	$25.00
____Northwest Weeds	
The Ugly and Beautiful Villains of Fields, Gardens, and Roadsides	$14.00
____OWLS Whoo are they?	$12.00
____Plants of Waterton-Glacier National Parks and the Northern Rockies	$12.00
____Roadside Plants of Southern California	$15.00
____Sagebrush Country A Wildflower Sanctuary	$14.00
____Sierra Nevada Wildflowers	$16.00
____Watchable Birds of California	$18.00
____Watchable Birds of the Great Basin	$16.00
____Watchable Birds of the Rocky Mountains	$14.00
____Watchable Birds of the Southwest	$14.00
____Wild Berries of the West	$16.00

Please include $3.00 per order to cover shipping and handling.

Send the books marked above. I enclose $_____

Name_____

Address_____

City/State/Zip_____

☐ Payment enclosed (check or money order in U.S. funds)

Bill my: ☐ VISA ☐ MasterCard ☐ Discover ☐ American Express

Expiration Date:_____

Card No._____

Signature _____

5 9 2 4 **Mountain Press Publishing Company**
P. O. Box 2399 • Missoula, MT 59806
Order Toll Free **1-800-234-5308** • *Have your credit card number ready.*
e-mail: mtnpress@montana.com • website: www.mountainpresspublish.com